The
MIRACLE
WORKER
and
MONDAY
AFTER THE
MIRACLE

The
MIRACLE
WORKER
and
MONDAY
AFTER THE
MIRACLE

WILLIAM GIBSON

Nelson Doubleday Inc. Garden City, New York

The
MIRACLE
WORKER

"At another time she asked, 'What is a soul?' 'No one knows,' I replied; 'but we know it is not the body, and it is that part of us which thinks and loves and hopes.' . . . [and] is invisible. . . . 'But if I write what my soul thinks,' she said, 'then it will be visible, and the words will be its body.' "

—ANNIE SULLIVAN, 1891

THE MIRACLE WORKER premiered at The Playhouse in New York City on October 19, 1959. It was directed by Arthur Penn, with scenery and lighting by George Jenkins and costumes by Ruth Morley.

The cast, in order of appearance, was as follows:

DOCTOR	*Roger De Koven*
KATE KELLER	*Patricia Neal*
CAPTAIN KELLER	*Torin Thatcher*
MARTHA	*Miriam Butler*
PERCY	*Caswell Fairweather*
VINEY	*Beah Richards*
HELEN KELLER	*Patty Duke*
JAMES KELLER	*James Congdon*
AUNT EV	*Kathleen Comegys*
ANAGNOS	*Michael Constantine*
ANNIE SULLIVAN	*Anne Bancroft*
CHILDREN:	*Lori Heineman, Dale Ellen Bethea, Rita Levy, Lynn Schoenfeld, Eileen Musumeci, Donna Pastore*
JOHN	*John Marriott*
MARY	*Juanita Bethea*

for the wife and the kids and the next breath
with love

THE PLAYING SPACE *is divided into two areas by a more or less diagonal line, which runs from downstage right to upstage left.*

THE AREA *behind this diagonal is on platforms and represents the Keller house; inside we see, down right, a family room, and up center, elevated, a bedroom. On stage level near center, outside a porch, there is a water pump.*

THE OTHER AREA, *in front of the diagonal, is neutral ground; it accommodates various places as designated at various times— the yard before the Keller home, the Perkins Institution for the Blind, the garden house, and so forth.*

THE CONVENTION OF THE STAGING *is one of cutting through time and place, and its essential qualities are fluidity and spatial counterpoint. To this end, the less set there is, the better; in a literal set, the fluidity will seem merely episodic. The stage therefore should be free, airy, unencumbered by walls. Apart from certain practical items—such as the pump, a window to climb out of, doors to be locked—locales should be only skeletal suggestions, and the movement from one to another should be accomplishable by little more than lights.*

CHARACTERS

A DOCTOR

KATE

KELLER

HELEN

MARTHA

PERCY

AUNT EV

JAMES

ANAGNOS

ANNIE SULLIVAN

VINEY

BLIND GIRLS

A SERVANT

OFFSTAGE VOICES

Time: The 1880's

Place: In and around the Keller homestead in Tuscumbia, Alabama; also, briefly, the Perkins Institution for the Blind, in Boston.

ACT ONE

ACT I

Inside, three adults in the bedroom are grouped around a crib, in lamplight. They have been through a long vigil, and it shows in their tired bearing and disarranged clothing. One is a young gentlewoman with a sweet girlish face, KATE KELLER; *the second is an elderly* DOCTOR, *stethoscope at neck, thermometer in fingers; the third is a hearty gentleman in his forties with chin whiskers,* CAPTAIN ARTHUR KELLER.

DOCTOR: She'll live.

KATE: Thank God.

(The DOCTOR *leaves them together over the crib, packs his bag.)*

DOCTOR: You're a pair of lucky parents. I can tell you now, I thought she wouldn't.

KELLER: Nonsense, the child's a Keller, she has the constitution of a goat. She'll outlive us all.

DOCTOR [AMIABLY]: Yes, especially if some of you Kellers don't get a night's sleep. I mean you, Mrs. Keller.

KELLER: You hear, Katie?

KATE: I hear.

KELLER [INDULGENT]: I've brought up two of them, but this is my wife's first, she isn't battle-scarred yet.

KATE: Doctor, don't be merely considerate, will my girl be all right?

DOCTOR: Oh, by morning she'll be knocking down Captain Keller's fences again.

KATE: And isn't there anything we should do?

KELLER [JOVIAL]: Put up stronger fencing, ha?

DOCTOR: Just let her get well, she knows how to do it better than we do.

(He is packed, ready to leave.)

Main thing is the fever's gone, these things come and go in infants, never know why. Call it acute congestion of the stomach and brain.

KELLER: I'll see you to your buggy, Doctor.

DOCTOR: I've never seen a baby, more vitality, that's the truth.

(He beams a good night at the baby and KATE, *and* KELLER *leads him downstairs with a lamp. They go down the porch steps, and across the yard, where the* DOCTOR *goes off left;* KELLER *stands with the lamp aloft.* KATE *meanwhile is bent lovingly over the crib, which emits a bleat; her finger is playful with the baby's face.)*

KATE: Hush. Don't you cry now, you've been trouble enough. Call it acute congestion, indeed, I don't see what's so cute about a congestion, just because it's yours. We'll have your father run an editorial in his paper, the wonders of modern medicine, they don't know what they're curing even when they cure it. Men, men and their battle scars, we women will have to—

(But she breaks off, puzzled, moves her finger before the baby's eyes.)

Will have to—Helen?

(Now she moves her hand, quickly.)

Helen.

(She snaps her fingers at the baby's eyes twice, and her hand falters; after a moment she calls out, loudly.)

Captain. Captain, will you come—

(But she stares at the baby, and her next call is directly at her ears.)

Captain!

(And now, still staring, KATE screams. KELLER in the yard hears it, and runs with the lamp back to the house. KATE screams again, her look intent on the baby and terrible. KELLER hurries in and up).

KELLER: Katie? What's wrong?

KATE: Look.

(She makes a pass with her hand in the crib, at the baby's eyes.)

KELLER: What, Katie? She's well, she needs only time to—

KATE: She can't see. Look at her eyes.

(She takes the lamp from him, moves it before the child's face.)

She can't *see!*

KELLER [HOARSELY]: Helen.

KATE: Or hear. When I screamed she didn't blink. Not an eyelash—

KELLER: Helen. Helen!

KATE: She can't *hear* you!

KELLER: *Helen!*

(His face has something like fury in it, crying the child's name; KATE almost fainting presses her knuckles to her mouth, to stop her own cry.

The room dims out quickly.)

Time, in the form of a slow tune of distant belfry chimes which approaches in a crescendo and then fades, passes; the light comes up again on a day five years later, on three kneeling children and an old dog outside around the pump.

The dog is a setter named BELLE, *and she is sleeping. Two of the children are Negroes,* MARTHA *and* PERCY. *The third child is* HELEN, *six and a half years old, quite unkempt, in body a vivacious little person with a fine head, attractive, but noticeably blind, one eye larger and protruding; her gestures are abrupt, insistent, lacking in human restraint, and her face never smiles. She is flanked by the other two, in a litter of paper-doll cutouts, and while they speak* HELEN'S *hands thrust at their faces in turn, feeling baffledly at the movements of their lips.)*

MARTHA [SNIPPING]: First I'm gonna cut off this doctor's legs, one, two, now then—

PERCY: Why you cuttin' off that doctor's legs?

MARTHA: I'm gonna give him a operation. Now I'm gonna cut off his arms, one, two. Now I'm gonna fix up—

(She pushes HELEN'S *hand away from her mouth.)*

You stop that.

PERCY: Cut off his stomach, that's a good operation.

MARTHA: No, I'm gonna cut off his head first, he got a bad cold.

PERCY: Ain't gonna be much of that doctor left to fix up, time you finish all them opera—

(But HELEN *is poking her fingers inside his mouth, to feel his tongue; he bites at them, annoyed, and she jerks them away.* HELEN *now fingers her own lips, moving them in imitation, but soundlessly.)*

MARTHA: What you do, bite her hand?

PERCY: That's how I do, she keep pokin' her fingers in my mouth, I just bite 'em off.

MARTHA: What she tryin' do now?

PERCY: She tryin' *talk*. She gonna get mad. Looka her tryin' talk.

(HELEN *is scowling, the lips under her fingertips moving in
ghostly silence, growing more and more frantic, until in a bi-
zarre rage she bites at her own fingers. This sends* PERCY *off into
laughter, but alarms* MARTHA.)

MARTHA: Hey, you stop now.

(*She pulls* HELEN'S *hand down.*)

You just sit quiet and—

(*But at once* HELEN *topples* MARTHA *on her back, knees pinning
her shoulders down, and grabs the scissors.* MARTHA *screams.*
PERCY *darts to the bell string on the porch, yanks it, and the bell
rings.*

*Inside, the lights have been gradually coming up on the main
room, where we see the family informally gathered, talking, but
in pantomime:* KATE *sits darning socks near a cradle, occasionally rocking it;* CAPTAIN KELLER *in spectacles is working over
newspaper pages at a table; a benign visitor in a hat,* AUNT EV, *is
sharing the sewing basket, putting the finishing touches on a big
shapeless doll made out of towels; an indolent young man,*
JAMES KELLER, *is at the window watching the children.*

With the ring of the bell, KATE *is instantly on her feet and out
the door onto the porch, to take in the scene; now we see what
these five years have done to her, the girlish playfulness is gone,
she is a woman steeled in grief.*)

KATE [FOR THE THOUSANDTH TIME]: Helen.

(*She is down the steps at once to them, seizing* HELEN'S *wrists
and lifting her off* MARTHA; MARTHA *runs off in tears and
screams for momma, with* PERCY *after her.*)

Let me have those scissors.

(Meanwhile the family inside is alerted, AUNT EV *joining* JAMES *at the window;* CAPTAIN KELLER *resumes work.)*

JAMES [BLANDLY]: She only dug Martha's eyes out. Almost dug. It's always almost, no point worrying till it happens, is there?

(They gaze out, while KATE *reaches for the scissors in* HELEN'S *hand. But* HELEN *pulls the scissors back, they struggle for them a moment, then* KATE *gives up, lets* HELEN *keep them. She tries to draw* HELEN *into the house.* HELEN *jerks away.* KATE *next goes down on her knees, takes* HELEN'S *hands gently, and using the scissors like a doll, makes* HELEN *caress and cradle them; she points* HELEN'S *finger housewards.* HELEN'S *whole body now becomes eager; she surrenders the scissors,* KATE *turns her toward the door and gives her a little push.* HELEN *scrambles up and toward the house, and* KATE *rising follows her.)*

AUNT EV: How does she stand it? Why haven't you seen this Baltimore man? It's not a thing you can let go on and on, like the weather.

JAMES: The weather here doesn't ask permission of me, Aunt Ev. Speak to my father.

AUNT EV: Arthur. Something ought to be done for that child.

KELLER: A refreshing suggestion. What?

*(KATE *entering turns* HELEN *to* AUNT EV, *who gives her the towel doll.)*

AUNT EV: Why, this very famous oculist in Baltimore I wrote you about, what was his name?

KATE: Dr. Chisholm.

AUNT EV: Yes, I heard lots of cases of blindness people thought couldn't be cured he's cured, he just does wonders. Why don't you write to him?

KELLER: I've stopped believing in wonders.

KATE [ROCKS THE CRADLE]: I think the Captain will write to him soon. Won't you, Captain?

KELLER: No.

JAMES [LIGHTLY]: Good money after bad, or bad after good. Or bad after bad—

AUNT EV: Well, if it's just a question of money, Arthur, now you're marshal you have this Yankee money. Might as well—

KELLER: Not money. The child's been to specialists all over Alabama and Tennessee, if I thought it would do good I'd have her to every fool doctor in the country.

KATE: I think the Captain will write to him soon.

KELLER: Katie. How many times can you let them break your heart?

KATE: Any number of times.

(HELEN *meanwhile sits on the floor to explore the doll with her fingers, and her hand pauses over the face: this is no face, a blank area of towel, and it troubles her. Her hand searches for features, and taps questioningly for eyes, but no one notices. She then yanks at her* AUNT'S *dress, and taps again vigorously for eyes.*)

AUNT EV: What, child?

(*Obviously not hearing,* HELEN *commences to go around, from person to person, tapping for eyes, but no one attends or understands.*)

KATE [NO BREAK]: As long as there's the least chance. For her to see. Or hear, or—

KELLER: There isn't. Now I must finish here.

KATE: I think, with your permission, Captain, I'd like to write.

KELLER: I said no, Katie.

AUNT EV: Why, writing does no harm, Arthur, only a little bitty letter. To see if he can help her.

KELLER: He can't.

KATE: We won't know that to be a fact, Captain, until after you write.

KELLER [RISING, EMPHATIC]: Katie, he can't.

(He collects his papers.)

JAMES [FACETIOUSLY]: Father stands up, that makes it a fact.

KELLER: You be quiet! I'm badgered enough here by females without your impudence.

(JAMES shuts up, makes himself scarce. HELEN now is groping among things on KELLER'S desk, and paws his papers to the floor. KELLER is exasperated.)

Katie.

(KATE quickly turns HELEN away, and retrieves the papers.)

I might as well try to work in a henyard as in this house—

JAMES [PLACATING]: You really ought to put her away, Father.

KATE [STARING UP]: What?

JAMES: Some asylum. It's the kindest thing.

AUNT EV: Why, she's your sister, James, not a nobody—

JAMES: Half sister, and half—mentally defective, she can't even keep herself clean. It's not pleasant to see her about all the time.

KATE: Do you dare? Complain of what you *can* see?

KELLER [VERY ANNOYED]: This discussion is at an end! I'll thank you not to broach it again, Ev.

(Silence descends at once. HELEN gropes her way with the doll, and KELLER turns back for a final word, explosive.)

I've done as much as I can bear, I can't give my whole life to it! The house is at sixes and sevens from morning till night over the child, it's time some attention was paid to Mildred here instead!

KATE [GENTLY DRY]: You'll wake her up, Captain.

KELLER: I want some peace in the house, I don't care how, but one way we won't have it is by rushing up and down the country every time someone hears of a new quack. I'm as sensible to this affliction as anyone else, it hurts me to look at the girl.

KATE: It was not our affliction I meant you to write about, Captain.

(HELEN *is back at* AUNT EV, *fingering her dress, and yanks two buttons from it.*)

AUNT EV: Helen! My buttons.

(HELEN *pushes the buttons into the doll's face.* KATE *now sees, comes swiftly to kneel, lifts* HELEN'S *hand to her own eyes in question.*)

KATE: Eyes?

(HELEN *nods energetically.*)

She wants the doll to have eyes.

(*Another kind of silence now, while* KATE *takes pins and buttons from the sewing basket and attaches them to the doll as eyes.* KELLER *stands, caught, and watches morosely.* AUNT EV *blinks, and conceals her emotion by inspecting her dress.*)

AUNT EV: My goodness me, I'm not decent.

KATE: She doesn't know better, Aunt Ev. I'll sew them on again.

JAMES: Never learn with everyone letting her do anything she takes it into her mind to—

KELLER: You be quiet!

JAMES: What did I say now?

KELLER: You talk too much.

JAMES: I was agreeing with you!

KELLER: Whatever it was. Deprived child, the least she can have are the little things she wants.

(JAMES, *very wounded, stalks out of the room onto the porch; he remains here, sulking.*)

AUNT EV [INDULGENTLY]: It's worth a couple of buttons, Kate, look.

(HELEN *now has the doll with eyes, and cannot contain herself for joy; she rocks the doll, pats it vigorously, kisses it.*)

This child has more sense than all these men Kellers, if there's ever any way to reach that mind of hers.

(*But* HELEN *suddenly has come upon the cradle, and unhesitatingly overturns it; the swaddled baby tumbles out, and* CAPTAIN KELLER *barely manages to dive and catch it in time.*)

KELLER: *Helen!*

(*All are in commotion, the baby screams, but* HELEN *unperturbed is laying her doll in its place.* KATE *on her knees pulls her hands off the cradle, wringing them;* HELEN *is bewildered.*)

KATE: Helen, Helen, you're not to do such things, how can I make you understand—

KELLER [HOARSELY]: Katie.

KATE: How can I get it into your head, my darling, my poor—

KELLER: Katie, some way of teaching her an iota of discipline has to be—

KATE [FLARING]: How can you discipline an afflicted child? Is it her fault?

(HELEN'S *fingers have fluttered to her* MOTHER'S *lips, vainly trying to comprehend their movements.*)

KELLER: I didn't say it was her fault.

KATE: Then whose? I don't know what to do! How can I teach her, beat her—until she's black and blue?

KELLER: It's not safe to let her run around loose. Now there must be a way of confining her, somehow, so she can't—

KATE: Where, in a cage? She's a growing child, she has to use her limbs!

KELLER: Answer me one thing, is it fair to Mildred here?

KATE [INEXORABLY]: Are you willing to put her away?

(Now HELEN'S *face darkens in the same rage as at herself earlier, and her hand strikes at* KATE'S *lips.* KATE *catches her hand again, and* HELEN *begins to kick, struggle, twist.)*

KELLER: Now what?

KATE: She wants to talk, like—*be* like you and me.

(She holds HELEN *struggling until we hear from the child her first sound so far, an inarticulate weird noise in her throat such as an animal in a trap might make; and* KATE *releases her. The second she is free* HELEN *blunders away, collides violently with a chair, falls, and sits weeping.* KATE *comes to her, embraces, caresses, soothes her, and buries her own face in her hair, until she can control her voice.)*

Every day she slips further away. And I don't know how to call her back.

AUNT EV: Oh, I've a mind to take her up to Baltimore myself. If that doctor can't help her, maybe he'll know who can.

KELLER [PRESENTLY, HEAVILY]: I'll write the man, Katie.

(He stands with the baby in his clasp, staring at HELEN'S *head, hanging down on* KATE'S *arm.*

The lights dim out, except the one on KATE *and* HELEN. *In the twilight,* JAMES, AUNT EV, *and* KELLER *move off slowly, formally, in separate directions;* KATE *with* HELEN *in her arms remains, motionless, in an image which overlaps into the next scene and fades only when it is well under way.*

Without pause, from the dark down left we hear a man's voice with a Greek accent speaking:)

ANAGNOS: —who could do nothing for the girl, of course. It was Dr. Bell who thought she might somehow be taught. I have written the family only that a suitable governess, Miss Annie Sullivan, has been found here in Boston—

(The lights begin to come up, down left, on a long table and chair. The table contains equipment for teaching the blind by touch—a small replica of the human skeleton, stuffed animals, models of flowers and plants, piles of books. The chair contains a girl of 20, ANNIE SULLIVAN, *with a face which in repose is grave and rather obstinate, and when active is impudent, combative, twinkling with all the life that is lacking in* HELEN'S, *and handsome; there is a crude vitality to her. Her suitcase is at her knee.* ANAGNOS, *a stocky bearded man, comes into the light only towards the end of his speech.)*

ANAGNOS: —and will come. It will no doubt be difficult for you there, Annie. But it has been difficult for you at our school too, hm? Gratifying, yes, when you came to us and could not spell your name, to accomplish so much here in a few years, but always an Irish battle. For independence.

(He studies ANNIE, *humorously; she does not open her eyes.)*

This is my last time to counsel you, Annie, and you do lack some —by some I mean *all*—what, tact or talent to bend. To others. And what has saved you on more than one occasion here at Perkins is that there was nowhere to expel you to. Your eyes hurt?

ANNIE: My ears, Mr. Anagnos.

(And now she has opened her eyes; they are inflamed, vague, slightly crossed, clouded by the granular growth of trachoma, and she often keeps them closed to shut out the pain of light.)

ANAGNOS [SEVERELY]: Nowhere but back to Tewksbury, where children learn to be saucy. Annie, I know how dreadful it was there, but that battle is dead and done with, why not let it stay buried?

ANNIE [CHEERILY]: I think God must owe me a resurrection.

ANAGNOS [A BIT SHOCKED]: What?

ANNIE [TAPS HER BROW]: Well, He keeps digging up that battle!

ANAGNOS: That is not a proper thing to say, Annie. It is what I mean.

ANNIE [MEEKLY]: Yes. But I know what I'm like, what's this child like?

ANAGNOS: Like?

ANNIE: Well— Bright or dull, to start off.

ANAGNOS: No one knows. And if she is dull, you have no patience with this?

ANNIE: Oh, in grownups you have to, Mr. Anagnos. I mean in children it just seems a little—precocious, can I use that word?

ANAGNOS: Only if you can spell it.

ANNIE: Premature. So I hope at least she's a bright one.

ANAGNOS: Deaf, blind, mute—who knows? She is like a little safe, locked, that no one can open. Perhaps there is a treasure inside.

ANNIE: Maybe it's empty, too?

ANAGNOS: Possible. I should warn you, she is much given to tantrums.

ANNIE: Means something is inside. Well, so am I, if I believe all I hear. Maybe you should warn *them*.

ANAGNOS [FROWNS]: Annie. I wrote them no word of your history. You will find yourself among strangers now, who know nothing of it.

ANNIE: Well, we'll keep them in a state of blessed ignorance.

ANAGNOS: Perhaps *you* should tell it?

ANNIE [BRISTLING]: Why? I have enough trouble with people who don't know.

ANAGNOS: So they will understand. When you have trouble.

ANNIE: The only time I have trouble is when I'm right.

(But she is amused at herself, as is ANAGNOS.*)*

Is it my fault it's so often? I won't give them trouble, Mr. Anagnos, I'll be so ladylike they won't notice I've come.

ANAGNOS: Annie, be—humble. It is not as if you have so many offers to pick and choose. You will need their affection, working with this child.

ANNIE [HUMOROUSLY]: I hope I won't need their pity.

ANAGNOS: Oh, we can all use some pity.

(Crisply)

So. You are no longer our pupil, we throw you into the world, a teacher. *If* the child can be taught. No one expects you to work miracles, even for twenty-five dollars a month. Now, in this envelope a loan, for the railroad, which you will repay me when you have a bank account. But in this box, a gift. With our love.

*(*ANNIE *opens the small box he extends, and sees a garnet ring. She looks up, blinking, and down.)*

I think other friends are ready to say goodbye.

(He moves as though to open doors.)

ANNIE: Mr. Anagnos.

(Her voice is trembling.)

Dear Mr. Anagnos, I—

(But she swallows over getting the ring on her finger, and cannot continue until she finds a woebegone joke.)

Well, what should I say, I'm an ignorant opinionated girl, and everything I am I owe to you?

ANAGNOS [SMILES]: That is only half true, Annie.

ANNIE: Which half? I crawled in here like a drowned rat, I thought I died when Jimmie died, that I'd never again—come alive. Well, you say with love so easy, and I haven't *loved* a soul since and I never will, I suppose, but this place gave me more than my eyes back. Or taught me how to spell, which I'll never learn anyway, but with all the fights and the trouble I've been here it taught me what help is, and how to live again, and I don't want to say goodbye. Don't open the door, I'm crying.

ANAGNOS [GENTLY]: They will not see.

(He moves again as though opening doors, and in comes a group of girls, 8-year-olds to 17-year-olds; as they walk we see they are blind. ANAGNOS shepherds them in with a hand.)

A CHILD: Annie?

ANNIE [HER VOICE CHEERFUL]: Here, Beatrice.

(As soon as they locate her voice they throng joyfully to her, speaking all at once; ANNIE is down on her knees to the smallest, and the following are the more intelligible fragments in the general hubbub.)

CHILDREN: There's a present. We brought you a going-away present, Annie!

ANNIE: Oh, now you shouldn't have—

CHILDREN: We did, we did, where's the present?

SMALLEST CHILD [MOURNFULLY]: Don't go, Annie, away.

CHILDREN: Alice has it. Alice! Where's Alice? Here I am! Where? Here!

(An arm is aloft out of the group, waving a present; ANNIE reaches for it.)

ANNIE: I have it. I have it, everybody, should I open it?

CHILDREN: Open it! Everyone be quiet! Do, Annie! She's opening it. Ssh!

(A settling of silence while ANNIE *unwraps it. The present is a pair of smoked glasses, and she stands still.)*

Is it open, Annie?

ANNIE: It's open.

CHILDREN: It's for your eyes, Annie. Put them on, Annie! 'Cause Mrs. Hopkins said your eyes hurt since the operation. And she said you're going where the sun is *fierce.*

ANNIE: I'm putting them on now.

SMALLEST CHILD [MOURNFULLY]: Don't go, Annie, where the sun is fierce.

CHILDREN: Do they fit all right?

ANNIE: Oh, they fit just fine.

CHILDREN: Did you put them on? Are they pretty, Annie?

ANNIE: Oh, my eyes feel hundreds of per cent better already, and pretty, why, do you know how I look in them? Splendiloquent. Like a race horse!

CHILDREN [DELIGHTED]: There's another present! Beatrice! We have a present for Helen, too! Give it to her, Beatrice. Here, Annie!

(This present is an elegant doll, with movable eyelids and a momma sound.)

It's for Helen. And we took up a collection to buy it. And Laura dressed it.

ANNIE: It's beautiful!

CHILDREN: So don't forget, you be sure to give it to Helen from us, Annie!

ANNIE: I promise it will be the first thing I give her. If I don't keep it for myself, that is, you know I can't be trusted with dolls!

SMALLEST CHILD [MOURNFULLY]: Don't go, Annie, to her.

ANNIE [HER ARM AROUND HER]: Sarah, dear. I don't *want* to go.

SMALLEST CHILD: Then why are you going?

ANNIE [GENTLY]: Because I'm a big girl now, and big girls have to earn a living. It's the only way I can. But if you don't smile for me first, what I'll just have to do is—

(She pauses, inviting it.)

SMALLEST CHILD: What?

ANNIE: Put *you* in my suitcase, instead of this doll. And take *you* to Helen in Alabama!

(This strikes the children as very funny, and they begin to laugh and tease the smallest child, who after a moment does smile for ANNIE.)

ANAGNOS [THEN]: Come, children. We must get the trunk into the carriage and Annie into her train, or no one will go to Alabama. Come, come.

(He shepherds them out and ANNIE *is left alone on her knees with the doll in her lap. She reaches for her suitcase, and by a subtle change in the color of the light, we go with her thoughts into another time. We hear a boy's voice whispering; perhaps we see shadowy intimations of these speakers in the background.)*

BOY'S VOICE: Where we goin', Annie?

ANNIE [IN DREAD]: Jimmie.

BOY'S VOICE: Where we goin'?

ANNIE: I said—I'm takin' care of you—

BOY'S VOICE: Forever and ever?

MAN'S VOICE [IMPERSONAL]: Annie Sullivan, aged nine, virtually blind. James Sullivan, aged seven—What's the matter with your leg, Sonny?

ANNIE: Forever and ever.

MAN'S VOICE: Can't he walk without that crutch?

(ANNIE *shakes her head, and does not stop shaking it.*)

Girl goes to the women's ward. Boy to the men's.

BOY'S VOICE [IN TERROR]: Annie! Annie, don't let them take me—Annie!

ANAGNOS [OFFSTAGE]: Annie! Annie?

(*But this voice is real, in the present, and* ANNIE *comes up out of her horror, clearing her head with a final shake; the lights begin to pick out* KATE *in the* KELLER *house, as* ANNIE *in a bright tone calls back.*)

ANNIE: Coming!

(*This word catches* KATE, *who stands half turned and attentive to it, almost as though hearing it. Meanwhile* ANNIE *turns and hurries out, lugging the suitcase.*

The room dims out; the sound of railroad wheels begins from off left, and maintains itself in a constant rhythm underneath the following scene; the remaining lights have come up on the KELLER *homestead.* JAMES *is lounging on the porch, waiting. In the upper bedroom which is to be* ANNIE'S, HELEN *is alone, puzzledly exploring, fingering and smelling things, the curtains, empty drawers in the bureau, water in the pitcher by the washbasin, fresh towels on the bedstead. Downstairs in the family room* KATE *turning to a mirror hastily adjusts her bonnet, watched by a Negro servant in an apron,* VINEY.)

VINEY: Let Mr. Jimmy go by hisself, you been pokin' that garden all day, you ought to rest your feet.

KATE: I can't wait to see her, Viney.

VINEY: Maybe she ain't gone be on this train neither.

KATE: Maybe she is.

VINEY: And maybe she ain't.

KATE: And maybe she is. Where's Helen?

VINEY: She upstairs, smellin' around. She know somethin' funny's goin' on.

KATE: Let her have her supper as soon as Mildred's in bed, and tell Captain Keller when he comes that we'll be delayed tonight.

VINEY: Again.

KATE: I don't think we need say *again*. Simply delayed will do.

(She runs upstairs to ANNIE'S *room,* VINEY *speaking after her.)*

VINEY: I mean that's what he gone say. "What, again?"

*(*VINEY *works at setting the table. Upstairs* KATE *stands in the doorway, watching* HELEN'S *groping explorations.)*

KATE: Yes, we're expecting someone. Someone for my Helen.

*(*HELEN *happens upon her skirt, clutches her leg;* KATE *in a tired dismay kneels to tidy her hair and soiled pinafore.)*

Oh, dear, this was clean not an hour ago.

*(*HELEN *feels her bonnet, shakes her head darkly, and tugs to get it off.* KATE *retains it with one hand, diverts* HELEN *by opening her other hand under her nose.)*

Here. For while I'm gone.

*(*HELEN *sniffs, reaches, and pops something into her mouth, while* KATE *speaks a bit guiltily.)*

I don't think one peppermint drop will spoil your supper.

(She gives HELEN *a quick kiss, evades her hands, and hurries downstairs again. Meanwhile* CAPTAIN KELLER *has entered the yard from around the rear of the house, newspaper under arm, cleaning off and munching on some radishes; he sees* JAMES *lounging at the porch post.)*

KELLER: Jimmie?

JAMES [UNMOVING]: Sir?

KELLER [EYES HIM]: You don't look dressed for anything useful, boy.

JAMES: I'm not. It's for Miss Sullivan.

KELLER: Needn't keep holding up that porch, we have wooden posts for that. I asked you to see that those strawberry plants were moved this evening.

JAMES: I'm moving your—Mrs. Keller, instead. To the station.

KELLER [HEAVILY]: Mrs. Keller. Must you always speak of her as though you haven't met the lady?

(KATE *comes out on the porch, and* JAMES *inclines his head.*)

JAMES [IRONIC]: Mother.

(*He starts off the porch, but sidesteps* KELLER'S *glare like a blow.*)

I said mother!

KATE: Captain.

KELLER: Evening, my dear.

KATE: We're off to meet the train, Captain. Supper will be a trifle delayed tonight.

KELLER: What, again?

KATE [BACKING OUT]: With your permission, Captain?

(*And they are gone.* KELLER *watches them offstage, morosely.*

Upstairs HELEN *meanwhile has groped for her mother, touched her cheek in a meaningful gesture, waited, touched her cheek, waited, then found the open door, and made her way down. Now she comes into the family room, touches her cheek again;* VINEY *regards her.*)

VINEY: What you want, honey, your momma?

(HELEN *touches her cheek again.* VINEY *goes to the sideboard, gets a tea-cake, gives it into* HELEN'S *hand;* HELEN *pops it into her mouth.*)

Guess one little tea-cake ain't gone ruin your appetite.

(She turns HELEN *toward the door.* HELEN *wanders out onto the porch, as* KELLER *comes up the steps. Her hands encounter him, and she touches her cheek again, waits.)*

KELLER: She's gone.

(He is awkward with her; when he puts his hand on her head, she pulls away. KELLER *stands regarding her, heavily.)*

She's gone, my son and I don't get along, you don't know I'm your father, no one likes me, and supper's delayed.

(HELEN *touches her cheek, waits.* KELLER *fishes in his pocket.)*

Here. I brought you some stick candy, one nibble of sweets can't do any harm.

(He gives her a large stick candy; HELEN *falls to it.* VINEY *peers out the window.)*

VINEY [REPROACHFULLY]: Cap'n Keller, now how'm I gone get her to eat her supper you fill her up with that trash?

KELLER [ROARS]: Tend to your work!

(VINEY *beats a rapid retreat.* KELLER *thinks better of it, and tries to get the candy away from* HELEN, *but* HELEN *hangs on to it; and when* KELLER *pulls, she gives his leg a kick.* KELLER *hops about,* HELEN *takes refuge with the candy down behind the pump, and* KELLER *then irately flings his newspaper on the porch floor, stamps into the house past* VINEY *and disappears.*

The lights half dim on the homestead, where VINEY *and* HELEN *going about their business soon find their way off. Meanwhile, the railroad sounds off left have mounted in a crescendo to a climax typical of a depot at arrival time, the lights come up on stage left, and we see a suggestion of a station. Here* ANNIE *in her smoked glasses and disarrayed by travel is waiting with her suitcase, while* JAMES *walks to meet her; she has a battered paper-bound book, which is a Perkins report, under her arm.)*

JAMES [COOLLY]: Miss Sullivan?

ANNIE [CHEERILY]: Here! At last, I've been on trains so many days I thought they must be backing up every time I dozed off—

JAMES: I'm James Keller.

ANNIE: James?

(The name stops her.)

I had a brother Jimmie. Are you Helen's?

JAMES: I'm only half a brother. You're to be her governess?

ANNIE [LIGHTLY]: Well. Try!

JAMES [EYING HER]: You look like half a governess.

*(*KATE *enters.* ANNIE *stands moveless, while* JAMES *takes her suitcase.* KATE'S *gaze on her is doubtful, troubled.)*

Mrs. Keller, Miss Sullivan.

*(*KATE *takes her hand.)*

KATE [SIMPLY]: We've met every train for two days.

*(*ANNIE *looks at* KATE'S *face, and her good humor comes back.)*

ANNIE: I changed trains every time they stopped, the man who sold me that ticket ought to be tied to the tracks—

JAMES: You have a trunk, Miss Sullivan?

ANNIE: Yes.

(She passes JAMES *a claim check, and he bears the suitcase out behind them.* ANNIE *holds the battered book.* KATE *is studying*

her face, and ANNIE *returns the gaze; this is a mutual appraisal, southern gentlewoman and working-class Irish girl, and* ANNIE *is not quite comfortable under it.)*

You didn't bring Helen, I was hoping you would.

KATE: No, she's home.

(A pause. ANNIE *tries to make ladylike small talk, though her energy now and then erupts; she catches herself up whenever she hears it.)*

ANNIE: You—live far from town, Mrs. Keller?

KATE: Only a mile.

ANNIE: Well. I suppose I can wait one more mile. But don't be surprised if I get out to push the horse!

KATE: Helen's waiting for you, too. There's been such a bustle in the house, she expects something, heaven knows what.

(Now she voices part of her doubt, not as such, but ANNIE *understands it.)*

I expected—a desiccated spinster. You're very young.

ANNIE [RESOLUTELY]: Oh, you should have seen me when I left Boston. I got much older on this trip.

KATE: I mean, to teach anyone as difficult as Helen.

ANNIE: *I* mean to try. They can't put you in jail for trying!

KATE: Is it possible, even? To teach a deaf-blind child *half* of what an ordinary child learns—has that ever been done?

ANNIE: Half?

KATE: A tenth.

ANNIE [RELUCTANTLY]: No.

*(*KATE'S *face loses its remaining hope, still appraising her youth.)*

Dr. Howe did wonders, but—an ordinary child? No, never. But then I thought when I was going over his reports—

(She indicates the one in her hand)

—he never treated them like ordinary children. More like— eggs everyone was afraid would break.

KATE [A PAUSE]: May I ask how old you are?

ANNIE: Well, I'm not in my teens, you know! I'm twenty.

KATE: All of twenty.

(ANNIE takes the bull by the horns, valiantly.)

ANNIE: Mrs. Keller, don't lose heart just because I'm not on my last legs. I have three big advantages over Dr. Howe that money couldn't buy for you. One is his work behind me, I've read every word he wrote about it and he wasn't exactly what you'd call a man of few words. Another is to *be* young, why, I've got energy to do anything. The third is, I've been blind.

(But it costs her something to say this.)

KATE [QUIETLY]: Advantages.

ANNIE [WRY]: Well, some have the luck of the Irish, some do not.

(KATE smiles; she likes her.)

KATE: What will you try to teach her first?

ANNIE: First, last, and—in between, language.

KATE: Language.

ANNIE: Language is to the mind more than light is to the eye. Dr. Howe said that.

KATE: Language.

(She shakes her head.)

We can't get through to teach her to sit still. You *are* young, despite your years, to have such—confidence. Do you, inside?

(ANNIE *studies her face; she likes her, too.*)

ANNIE: No, to tell you the truth I'm as shaky inside as a baby's rattle!

(*They smile at each other, and* KATE *pats her hand.*)

KATE: Don't be.

(JAMES *returns to usher them off.*)

We'll do all we can to help, and to make you feel at home. Don't think of us as strangers, Miss Annie.

ANNIE [CHEERILY]: Oh, strangers aren't so strange to me. I've known them all my life!

(KATE *smiles again,* ANNIE *smiles back, and they precede* JAMES *offstage.*

The lights dim on them, having simultaneously risen full on the house; VINEY *has already entered the family room, taken a water pitcher, and come out and down to the pump. She pumps real water. As she looks offstage, we hear the clop of hoofs, a carriage stopping, and voices.*)

VINEY: Cap'n Keller! Cap'n Keller, they comin'!

(*She goes back into the house, as* KELLER *comes out on the porch to gaze.*)

She sure 'nuff came, Cap'n.

(KELLER *descends, and crosses toward the carriage; this conversation begins offstage and moves on.*)

KELLER [VERY COURTLY]: Welcome to Ivy Green, Miss Sullivan. I take it you are Miss Sullivan—

KATE: My husband, Miss Annie, Captain Keller.

ANNIE [HER BEST BEHAVIOR]: Captain, how do you do.

KELLER: A pleasure to see you, at last. I trust you had an agreeable journey?

ANNIE: Oh, I had several! When did this country get so big?

JAMES: Where would you like the trunk, father?

KELLER: Where Miss Sullivan can get at it, I imagine.

ANNIE: Yes, please. Where's Helen?

KELLER: In the hall, Jimmie—

KATE: We've put you in the upstairs corner room, Miss Annie, if there's any breeze at all this summer, you'll feel it—

(In the house the setter BELLE *flees into the family room, pursued by* HELEN *with groping hands; the dog doubles back out the same door, and* HELEN *still groping for her makes her way out to the porch; she is messy, her hair tumbled, her pinafore now ripped, her shoelaces untied.* KELLER *acquires the suitcase, and* ANNIE *gets her hands on it too, though still endeavoring to live up to the general air of propertied manners.)*

KELLER: *And* the suitcase—

ANNIE [PLEASANTLY]: I'll take the suitcase, thanks.

KELLER: Not at all, I have it, Miss Sullivan.

ANNIE: I'd like it.

KELLER [GALLANTLY]: I couldn't think of it, Miss Sullivan. You'll find in the south we—

ANNIE: Let me.

KELLER: —view women as the flowers of civiliza—

ANNIE [IMPATIENTLY]: I've got something in it for Helen!

(She tugs it free; KELLER *stares.)*

Thank you. When do I see her?

KATE: There. There is Helen.

(ANNIE *turns, and sees* HELEN *on the porch. A moment of silence. Then* ANNIE *begins across the yard to her, lugging her suitcase.*)

KELLER [SOTTO VOCE]: Katie—

(KATE *silences him with a hand on his arm. When* ANNIE *finally reaches the porch steps she stops, contemplating* HELEN *for a last moment before entering her world. Then she drops the suitcase on the porch with intentional heaviness,* HELEN *starts with the jar, and comes to grope over it.* ANNIE *puts forth her hand, and touches* HELEN'S. HELEN *at once grasps it, and commences to explore it, like reading a face. She moves her hand on to* ANNIE'S *forearm, and dress; and* ANNIE *brings her face within reach of* HELEN'S *fingers, which travel over it, quite without timidity, until they encounter and push aside the smoked glasses.* ANNIE'S *gaze is grave, unpitying, very attentive. She puts her hands on* HELEN'S *arms, but* HELEN *at once pulls away, and they confront each other with a distance between. Then* HELEN *returns to the suitcase, tries to open it, cannot.* ANNIE *points* HELEN'S *hand overhead.* HELEN *pulls away, tries to open the suitcase again;* ANNIE *points her hand overhead again.* HELEN *points overhead, a question, and* ANNIE, *drawing* HELEN'S *hand to her own face, nods.* HELEN *now begins tugging the suitcase toward the door; when* ANNIE *tries to take it from her, she fights her off and backs through the doorway with it.* ANNIE *stands a moment, then follows her in, and together they get the suitcase up the steps into* ANNIE'S *room.*)

KATE: Well?

KELLER: She's very rough, Katie.

KATE: I like her, Captain.

KELLER: Certainly rear a peculiar kind of young woman in the north. How old is she?

KATE [VAGUELY]: Ohh— Well, she's not in her teens, you know.

KELLER: She's only a child. What's her family like, shipping her off alone this far?

KATE: I couldn't learn. She's very closemouthed about some things.

KELLER: Why does she wear those glasses? I like to see a person's eyes when I talk to—

KATE: For the sun. She was blind.

KELLER: Blind.

KATE: She's had nine operations on her eyes. One just before she left.

KELLER: Blind, good heavens, do they expect one blind child to teach another? Has she experience at least, how long did she teach there?

KATE: She was a pupil.

KELLER [HEAVILY]: Katie, Katie. This is her first position?

KATE [BRIGHT VOICE]: She was valedictorian—

KELLER: Here's a houseful of grownups can't cope with the child, how can an inexperienced half-blind Yankee schoolgirl manage her?

(JAMES *moves in with the trunk on his shoulder.*)

JAMES [EASILY]: Great improvement. Now we have two of them to look after.

KELLER: You look after those strawberry plants!

(JAMES *stops with the trunk.* KELLER *turns from him without another word, and marches off.*)

JAMES: Nothing I say is right.

KATE: Why say anything?

(She calls.)

Don't be long, Captain, we'll have supper right away—

(She goes into the house, and through the rear door of the family room. JAMES *trudges in with the trunk, takes it up the steps to* ANNIE'S *room, and sets it down outside the door. The lights elsewhere dim somewhat.*

Meanwhile, inside, ANNIE *has given* HELEN *a key; while* ANNIE *removes her bonnet,* HELEN *unlocks and opens the suitcase. The first thing she pulls out is a voluminous shawl. She fingers it until she perceives what it is; then she wraps it around her, and acquiring* ANNIE'S *bonnet and smoked glasses as well, dons the lot: the shawl swamps her, and the bonnet settles down upon the glasses, but she stands before a mirror cocking her head to one side, then to the other, in a mockery of adult action.* ANNIE *is amused, and talks to her as one might to a kitten, with no trace of company manners.)*

ANNIE: All the trouble I went to and that's how I look?

*(*HELEN *then comes back to the suitcase, gropes for more, lifts out a pair of female drawers.)*

Oh, no. Not the drawers!

(But HELEN *discarding them comes to the elegant doll. Her fingers explore its features, and when she raises it and finds its eyes open and close, she is at first startled, then delighted. She picks it up, taps its head vigorously, taps her own chest, and nods questioningly.* ANNIE *takes her finger, points it to the doll, points it to* HELEN, *and touching it to her own face, also nods.* HELEN *sits back on her heels, clasps the doll to herself, and rocks it.* ANNIE *studies her, still in bonnet and smoked glasses like a caricature of herself, and addresses her humorously.)*

All right, Miss O'Sullivan. Let's begin with doll.

(She takes HELEN'S *hand; in her palm* ANNIE'S *forefinger points, thumb holding her other fingers clenched.)*

D.

(Her thumb next holds all her fingers clenched, touching HELEN'S *palm.)*

O.

(Her thumb and forefinger extend.)

L.

(Same contact repeated.)

L.

(She puts HELEN'S *hand to the doll.)*

Doll.

JAMES: You spell pretty well.

*(*ANNIE *in one hurried move gets the drawers swiftly back into the suitcase, the lid banged shut, and her head turned, to see* JAMES *leaning in the doorway.)*

Finding out if she's ticklish? She is.

*(*ANNIE *regards him stonily, but* HELEN *after a scowling moment tugs at her hand again, imperious.* ANNIE *repeats the letters, and* HELEN *interrupts her fingers in the middle, feeling each of them, puzzled.* ANNIE *touches* HELEN'S *hand to the doll, and begins spelling into it again.)*

JAMES: What is it, a game?

ANNIE [CURTLY]: An alphabet.

JAMES: Alphabet?

ANNIE: For the deaf.

*(*HELEN *now repeats the finger movements in air, exactly, her head cocked to her own hand, and* ANNIE'S *eyes suddenly gleam.)*

Ho. How *bright* she is!

JAMES: You think she knows what she's doing?

(He takes HELEN'S *hand, to throw a meaningless gesture into it; she repeats this one too.)*

She imitates everything, she's a monkey.

ANNIE [VERY PLEASED]: Yes, she's a bright little monkey, all right.

(She takes the doll from HELEN, *and reaches for her hand;* HELEN *instantly grabs the doll back.* ANNIE *takes it again, and* HELEN'S *hand next, but* HELEN *is incensed now; when* ANNIE *draws her hand to her face to shake her head no, then tries to spell to her,* HELEN *slaps at* ANNIE'S *face.* ANNIE *grasps* HELEN *by both arms, and swings her into a chair, holding her pinned there, kicking, while glasses, doll, bonnet fly in various directions.* JAMES *laughs.)*

JAMES: She wants her doll back.

ANNIE: When she spells it.

JAMES: Spell, she doesn't know the thing has a name, even.

ANNIE: Of course not, who expects her to, now? All I want is her fingers to learn the letters.

JAMES: Won't mean anything to her.

*(*ANNIE *gives him a look. She then tries to form* HELEN'S *fingers into the letters, but* HELEN *swings a haymaker instead, which* ANNIE *barely ducks, at once pinning her down again.)*

Doesn't like that alphabet, Miss Sullivan. You invent it yourself?

*(*HELEN *is now in a rage, fighting tooth and nail to get out of the chair, and* ANNIE *answers while struggling and dodging her kicks.)*

ANNIE: Spanish monks under a—vow of silence. Which I wish *you'd* take!

(And suddenly releasing HELEN'S *hands, she comes and shuts the door in* JAMES' *face.* HELEN *drops to the floor, groping around for the doll.* ANNIE *looks around desperately, sees her purse on the bed, rummages in it, and comes up with a battered piece of cake wrapped in newspaper; with her foot she moves the doll deftly out of the way of* HELEN'S *groping, and going on her knee she lets* HELEN *smell the cake. When* HELEN *grabs for it,* ANNIE *removes the cake and spells quickly into the reaching hand.)*

Cake. From Washington up north, it's the best I can do.

*(*HELEN'S *hand waits, baffled.* ANNIE *repeats it.)*

C, a, k, e. Do what my fingers do, never mind what it means.

(She touches the cake briefly to HELEN'S *nose, pats her hand, presents her own hand.* HELEN *spells the letters rapidly back.* ANNIE *pats her hand enthusiastically, and gives her the cake;* HELEN *crams it into her mouth with both hands.* ANNIE *watches her, with humor.)*

Get it down fast, maybe I'll steal that back too. Now.

(She takes the doll, touches it to HELEN'S *nose, and spells again into her hand.)*

D, o, l, l. Think it over.

*(*HELEN *thinks it over, while* ANNIE *presents her own hand. Then* HELEN *spells three letters.* ANNIE *waits a second, then completes the word for* HELEN *in her palm.)*

L.

(She hands over the doll, and HELEN *gets a good grip on its leg.)*

Imitate now, understand later. End of the first les—

(She never finishes, because HELEN *swings the doll with a furious energy, it hits* ANNIE *squarely in the face, and she falls back*

with a cry of pain, her knuckles up to her mouth. HELEN *waits, tensed for further combat. When* ANNIE *lowers her knuckles she looks at blood on them; she works her lips, gets to her feet, finds the mirror, and bares her teeth at herself. Now she is furious herself.)*

You little wretch, no one's taught you *any* manners? I'll—

(But rounding from the mirror she sees the door slam, HELEN *and the doll are on the outside, and* HELEN *is turning the key in the lock.* ANNIE *darts over, to pull the knob; the door is locked fast. She yanks it again.)*

Helen! Helen, let me out of—

(She bats her brow at the folly of speaking, but JAMES, *now downstairs, hears her and turns to see* HELEN *with the key and doll groping her way down the steps;* JAMES *takes in the whole situation, makes a move to intercept* HELEN, *but then changes his mind, lets her pass, and amusedly follows her out onto the porch. Upstairs* ANNIE *meanwhile rattles the knob, kneels, peers through the keyhole, gets up. She goes to the window, looks down, frowns.* JAMES *from the yard sings gaily up to her:)*

JAMES:

*Buffalo girl, are you coming out tonight,
Coming out tonight,
Coming out—*

(He drifts back into the house. ANNIE *takes a handkerchief, nurses her mouth, stands in the middle of the room, staring at door and window in turn, and so catches sight of herself in the mirror, her cheek scratched, her hair dishevelled, her handkerchief bloody, her face disgusted with herself. She addresses the mirror, with some irony.)*

ANNIE: Don't worry. They'll find you, you're not lost. Only out of place.

(But she coughs, spits something into her palm, and stares at it, outraged.)

And toothless.

(She winces.)

Oo! It hurts.

(She pours some water into the basin, dips the handkerchief, and presses it to her mouth. Standing there, bent over the basin in pain—with the rest of the set dim and unreal, and the lights upon her taking on the subtle color of the past—she hears again, as do we, the faraway voices, and slowly she lifts her head to them; the boy's voice is the same, the others are cracked old crones in a nightmare, and perhaps we see their shadows.)

BOY'S VOICE: It hurts. Annie, it hurts.

FIRST CRONE'S VOICE: Keep that brat shut up, can't you, girlie, how's a body to get any sleep in this damn ward?

BOY'S VOICE: It hurts. It hurts.

SECOND CRONE'S VOICE: Shut up, you!

BOY'S VOICE: Annie, when are we goin' home? You promised!

ANNIE: Jimmie—

BOY'S VOICE: Forever and ever, you said forever—

(ANNIE *drops the handkerchief, averts to the window, and is arrested there by the next cry.)*

Annie? Annie, you there? Annie! It *hurts!*

THIRD CRONE'S VOICE: Grab him, he's fallin'!

BOY'S VOICE: *Annie!*

DOCTOR'S VOICE [A PAUSE, SLOWLY]: Little girl. Little girl, I must tell you your brother will be going on a—

(But ANNIE *claps her hands to her ears, to shut this out; there is instant silence.*

As the lights bring the other areas in again, JAMES *goes to the steps to listen for any sound from upstairs.* KELLER *re-entering from left crosses toward the house; he passes* HELEN *en route to her retreat under the pump.* KATE *re-enters the rear door of the family room, with flowers for the table.)*

KATE: Supper is ready, Jimmie, will you call your father?

JAMES: Certainly.

(But he calls up the stairs, for ANNIE'S *benefit:)*

Father! Supper!

KELLER [AT THE DOOR]: No need to shout, I've been cooling my heels for an hour. Sit down.

JAMES: Certainly.

KELLER: Viney!

(VINEY backs in with a roast, while they get settled around the table.)

VINEY: Yes, Cap'n, right here.

KATE: Mildred went directly to sleep, Viney?

VINEY: Oh yes, that babe's a angel.

KATE: And Helen had a good supper?

VINEY [VAGUELY]: I dunno, Miss Kate, somehow she didn't have much of a appetite tonight—

KATE [A BIT GUILTY]: Oh. Dear.

KELLER [HASTILY]: Well, now. Couldn't say the same for my part, I'm famished. Katie, your plate.

KATE [LOOKING]: But where is Miss Annie?

(A silence.)

JAMES [PLEASANTLY]: In her room.

KELLER: In her room? Doesn't she know hot food must be eaten hot? Go bring her down at once, Jimmie.

JAMES [RISES]: Certainly. I'll get a ladder.

KELLER [STARES]: What?

JAMES: I'll need a ladder. Shouldn't take me long.

KATE [STARES]: What shouldn't take you—

KELLER: Jimmie, do as I say! Go upstairs at once and tell Miss Sullivan supper is getting cold—

JAMES: She's locked in her room.

KELLER: Locked in her—

KATE: What on earth are you—

JAMES: Helen locked her in and made off with the key.

KATE [RISING]: And you sit here and say nothing?

JAMES: Well, everyone's been telling me not to say anything.

(He goes serenely out and across the yard, whistling. KELLER *thrusting up from his chair makes for the stairs.)*

KATE: Viney, look out in back for Helen. See if she has that key.

VINEY: Yes, Miss Kate.

(VINEY goes out the rear door.)

KELLER [CALLING DOWN]: She's out by the pump!

(KATE goes out on the porch after HELEN, *while* KELLER *knocks on* ANNIE'S *door, then rattles the knob, imperiously.)*

Miss Sullivan! Are you in there?

ANNIE: Oh, I'm in here, all right.

KELLER: Is there no key on your side?

ANNIE [WITH SOME ASPERITY]: Well, if there was a key in here, *I* wouldn't be in here. Helen took it, the only thing on my side is me.

KELLER: Miss Sullivan. I—

(He tries, but cannot hold it back.)

Not in the house ten minutes, I don't see *how* you managed it!

(He stomps downstairs again, while ANNIE *mutters to herself.)*

ANNIE: And even I'm not on my side.

KELLER [ROARING]: Viney!

VINEY [REAPPEARING]: Yes, Cap'n?

KELLER: Put that meat back in the oven!

*(*VINEY *bears the roast off again, while* KELLER *strides out onto the porch.* KATE *is with* HELEN *at the pump, opening her hands.)*

KATE: She has no key.

KELLER: Nonsense, she must have the key. Have you searched in her pockets?

KATE: Yes. She doesn't have it.

KELLER: Katie, she must have the key.

KATE: Would you prefer to search her yourself, Captain?

KELLER: No, I would not prefer to search her! She almost took my kneecap off this evening, when I tried merely to—

*(*JAMES *reappears carrying a long ladder, with* PERCY *running after him to be in on things.)*

Take that ladder back!

JAMES: Certainly.

(He turns around with it. MARTHA *comes skipping around the upstage corner of the house to be in on things, accompanied by the setter* BELLE.*)*

KATE: She could have hidden the key.

KELLER: Where?

KATE: Anywhere. Under a stone. In the flower beds. In the grass—

KELLER: Well, I can't plow up the entire grounds to find a missing key! Jimmie!

JAMES: Sir?

KELLER: Bring me a ladder!

JAMES: Certainly.

(VINEY *comes around the downstage side of the house to be in on things; she has* MILDRED *over her shoulder, bleating.* KELLER *places the ladder against* ANNIE'S *window and mounts.* ANNIE *meanwhile is running about making herself presentable, washing the blood off her mouth, straightening her clothes, tidying her hair. Another Negro servant enters to gaze in wonder, increasing the gathering ring of spectators.)*

KATE [SHARPLY]: What is Mildred doing up?

VINEY: Cap'n woke her, ma'am, all that hollerin'.

KELLER: Miss Sullivan!

(ANNIE *comes to the window, with as much air of gracious normality as she can manage;* KELLER *is at the window.)*

ANNIE [BRIGHTLY]: Yes, Captain Keller?

KELLER: Come out!

ANNIE: I don't see how I can. There isn't room.

KELLER: I intend to carry you. Climb onto my shoulder and hold tight.

ANNIE: Oh, no. It's—very chivalrous of you, but I'd really prefer to—

KELLER: Miss Sullivan, follow instructions! I will not have you also tumbling out of our windows.

(ANNIE *obeys, with some misgivings.*)

I hope this is not a sample of what we may expect from you. In the way of simplifying the work of looking after Helen.

ANNIE: Captain Keller, I'm perfectly able to go down a ladder under my own—

KELLER: I doubt it, Miss Sullivan. Simply hold onto my neck.

(*He begins down with her, while the spectators stand in a wide and somewhat awe-stricken circle, watching.* KELLER *half-misses a rung, and* ANNIE *grabs at his whiskers.*)

My *neck,* Miss Sullivan!

ANNIE: I'm sorry to inconvenience you this way—

KELLER: No inconvenience, other than having that door taken down and the lock replaced, if we fail to find that key.

ANNIE: Oh, I'll look everywhere for it.

KELLER: Thank you. Do not look in any rooms that can be locked. There.

(*He stands her on the ground.* JAMES *applauds.*)

ANNIE: Thank you very much.

(*She smooths her skirt, looking as composed and ladylike as possible.* KELLER *stares around at the spectators.*)

KELLER: Go, go, back to your work. What are you looking at here? There's nothing here to look at.

(*They break up, move off.*)

Now would it be possible for us to have supper, like other people?

(*He marches into the house.*)

KATE: Viney, serve supper. I'll put Mildred to sleep.

(They all go in. JAMES *is the last to leave, murmuring to* ANNIE *with a gesture.)*

JAMES: Might as well leave the l, a, d, d, e, r, hm?

*(*ANNIE *ignores him, looking at* HELEN; JAMES *goes in too. Imperceptibly the lights commence to narrow down.* ANNIE *and* HELEN *are now alone in the yard,* HELEN *seated at the pump, where she has been oblivious to it all, a battered little savage, playing with the doll in a picture of innocent contentment.* ANNIE *comes near, leans against the house, and taking off her smoked glasses, studies her, not without awe. Presently* HELEN *rises, gropes around to see if anyone is present;* ANNIE *evades her hand, and when* HELEN *is satisfied she is alone, the key suddenly protrudes out of her mouth. She takes it in her fingers, stands thinking, gropes to the pump, lifts a loose board, drops the key into the well, and hugs herself gleefully.* ANNIE *stares. But after a moment she shakes her head to herself, she cannot keep the smile from her lips.)*

ANNIE: You *devil.*

(Her tone is one of great respect, humor, and acceptance of challenge.)

You think I'm so easily gotten rid of? You have a thing or two to learn, first. I have nothing else to do.

(She goes up the steps to the porch, but turns for a final word, almost of warning.)

And nowhere to go.

(And presently she moves into the house to the others, as the lights dim down and out, except for the small circle upon HELEN *solitary at the pump, which ends the act.)*

ACT TWO

ACT II

IT IS EVENING.

The only room visible in the KELLER *house is* ANNIE'S, *where by lamplight* ANNIE *in a shawl is at a desk writing a letter; at her bureau* HELEN *in her customary unkempt state is tucking her doll in the bottom drawer as a cradle, the contents of which she has dumped out, creating as usual a fine disorder.*

ANNIE *mutters each word as she writes her letter, slowly, her eyes close to and almost touching the page, to follow with difficulty her penwork.*

ANNIE: ". . . and, nobody, here, has, attempted, to, control, her. The, greatest, problem, I, have, is, how, to, disipline, her, without, breaking, her, spirit."

(Resolute voice)

"But, I, shall, insist, on, reasonable, obedience, from, the, start—"

(At which point HELEN, *groping about on the desk, knocks over the inkwell.* ANNIE *jumps up, rescues her letter, rights the inkwell, grabs a towel to stem the spillage, and then wipes at* HELEN'S *hands;* HELEN *as always pulls free, but not until* ANNIE *first gets three letters into her palm.)*

Ink.

(HELEN is enough interested in and puzzled by this spelling that she proffers her hand again; so ANNIE *spells and impassively dunks it back in the spillage.)*

Ink. It has a name.

(She wipes the hand clean, and leads HELEN *to her bureau, where she looks for something to engage her. She finds a sewing card, with needle and thread, and going to her knees, shows* HELEN'S *hand how to connect one row of holes.)*

Down. Under. Up. And be careful of the needle—

*(*HELEN *gets it, and* ANNIE *rises.)*

Fine. You keep out of the ink and perhaps I can keep out of—the soup.

(She returns to the desk, tidies it, and resumes writing her letter, bent close to the page.)

"These, blots, are, her, handiwork. I—"

(She is interrupted by a gasp: HELEN *has stuck her finger, and sits sucking at it, darkly. Then with vengeful resolve she seizes her doll, and is about to dash its brains out on the floor when* ANNIE *diving catches it in one hand, which she at once shakes with hopping pain but otherwise ignores, patiently.)*

All right, let's try temperance.

(Taking the doll, she kneels, goes through the motion of knocking its head on the floor, spells into HELEN'S *hand:)*

Bad, girl.

(She lets HELEN *feel the grieved expression on her face.* HELEN *imitates it. Next she makes* HELEN *caress the doll and kiss the hurt spot and hold it gently in her arms, then spells into her hand:)*

Good, girl.

(She lets HELEN *feel the smile on her face.* HELEN *sits with a scowl, which suddenly clears; she pats the doll, kisses it,*

wreathes her face in a large artificial smile, and bears the doll to the washstand, where she carefully sits it. ANNIE *watches, pleased.)*

Very good girl—

(Whereupon HELEN *elevates the pitcher and dashes it on the floor instead.* ANNIE *leaps to her feet, and stands inarticulate;* HELEN *calmly gropes back to sit to the sewing card and needle.*

ANNIE *manages to achieve self-control. She picks up a fragment or two of the pitcher, sees* HELEN *is puzzling over the card, and resolutely kneels to demonstrate it again. She spells into* HELEN'S *hand.*

KATE *meanwhile coming around the corner with folded sheets on her arm, halts at the doorway and watches them for a moment in silence; she is moved, but level.)*

KATE [PRESENTLY]: What are you saying to her?

*(*ANNIE *glancing up is a bit embarrassed, and rises from the spelling, to find her company manners.)*

ANNIE: Oh, I was just making conversation. Saying it was a sewing card.

KATE: But does that—

(She imitates with her fingers)

—mean that to her?

ANNIE: No. No, she won't know what spelling is till she knows what a word is.

KATE: Yet you keep spelling to her. Why?

ANNIE [CHEERILY]: I like to hear myself talk!

KATE: The Captain says it's like spelling to the fence post.

ANNIE [A PAUSE]: Does he, now.

KATE: Is it?

ANNIE: No, it's how I watch you talk to Mildred.

KATE: Mildred.

ANNIE: Any baby. Gibberish, grown-up gibberish, baby-talk gibberish, do they understand one word of it to start? Somehow they begin to. If they hear it, I'm letting Helen hear it.

KATE: Other children are not—impaired.

ANNIE: Ho, there's nothing impaired in that head, it works like a mousetrap!

KATE [SMILES]: But after a child hears how many words, Miss Annie, a million?

ANNIE: I guess no mother's ever minded enough to count.

(She drops her eyes to spell into HELEN's *hand, again indicating the card;* HELEN *spells back, and* ANNIE *is amused.)*

KATE [TOO QUICKLY]: What did she spell?

ANNIE: I spelt card. She spelt cake!

(She takes in KATE's *quickness, and shakes her head, gently.)*

No, it's only a finger-game to her, Mrs. Keller. What she has to learn first is that things have names.

KATE: And when will she learn?

ANNIE: Maybe after a million and one words.

(They hold each other's gaze; KATE *then speaks quietly.)*

KATE: I should like to learn those letters, Miss Annie.

ANNIE [PLEASED]: I'll teach you tomorrow morning. That makes only half a million each!

KATE [THEN]: It's her bedtime.

*(*ANNIE *reaches for the sewing card,* HELEN *objects,* ANNIE *insists, and* HELEN *gets rid of* ANNIE's *hand by jabbing it with the*

needle. ANNIE *gasps, and moves to grip* HELEN'S *wrist; but* KATE *intervenes with a proffered sweet, and* HELEN *drops the card, crams the sweet into her mouth, and scrambles up to search her mother's hands for more.* ANNIE *nurses her wound, staring after the sweet.)*

I'm sorry, Miss Annie.

ANNIE [INDIGNANTLY]: Why does she get a reward? For stabbing me?

KATE: Well—

(Then, tiredly)

We catch our flies with honey, I'm afraid. We haven't the heart for much else, and so many times she simply cannot be compelled.

ANNIE [OMINOUS]: Yes. I'm the same way myself.

(KATE smiles, and leads HELEN *off around the corner.* ANNIE *alone in her room picks up things and in the act of removing* HELEN'S *doll gives way to unmannerly temptation: she throttles it. She drops it on her bed, and stands pondering. Then she turns back, sits decisively, and writes again, as the lights dim on her.)*

(Grimly)

"The, more, I, think, the, more, certain, I, am, that, obedience, is, the, gateway, through, which, knowledge, enters, the, mind, of, the, child—"

(On the word "obedience" a shaft of sunlight hits the water pump outside, while ANNIE'S *voice ends in the dark, followed by a distant cockcrow; daylight comes up over another corner of the sky, with* VINEY'S *voice heard at once.)*

VINEY: Breakfast ready!

(VINEY comes down into the sunlight beam, and pumps a pitcherful of water. While the pitcher is brimming we hear conversa-

tion from the dark; the light grows to the family room of the house where all are either entering or already seated at breakfast, with KELLER *and* JAMES *arguing the war.* HELEN *is wandering around the table to explore the contents of the other plates. When* ANNIE *is in her chair, she watches* HELEN. VINEY *re-enters, sets the pitcher on the table;* KATE *lifts the almost empty biscuit plate with an inquiring look,* VINEY *nods and bears it off back, neither of them interrupting the men.* ANNIE *meanwhile sits with fork quiet, watching* HELEN, *who at her mother's plate pokes her hand among some scrambled eggs.* KATE *catches* ANNIE'S *eyes on her, smiles with a wry gesture.* HELEN *moves on to* JAMES'S *plate, the male talk continuing,* JAMES *deferential and* KELLER *overriding.)*

JAMES: —no, but shouldn't we give the devil his due, father? The fact is we lost the South two years earlier when he outthought us behind Vicksburg.

KELLER: Outthought is a peculiar word for a butcher.

JAMES: Harness maker, wasn't he?

KELLER: I said butcher, his only virtue as a soldier was numbers and he led them to slaughter with no more regard than for so many sheep.

JAMES: But even if in that sense he was a butcher, the fact is he—

KELLER: And a drunken one, half the war.

JAMES: Agreed, father. If his own people said he was I can't argue he—

KELLER: Well, what is it you find to admire in such a man, Jimmie, the butchery or the drunkenness?

JAMES: Neither, father, only the fact that he beat us.

KELLER: He didn't.

JAMES: Is it your contention we won the war, sir?

KELLER: He didn't beat us at Vicksburg. We lost Vicksburg because Pemberton gave Bragg five thousand of his cavalry and Loring, whom I knew personally for a nincompoop before you were born, marched away from Champion's Hill with enough men to have held them, we lost Vicksburg by stupidity verging on treason.

JAMES: I would have said we lost Vicksburg because Grant was one thing no Yankee general was before him—

KELLER: Drunk? I doubt it.

JAMES: Obstinate.

KELLER: Obstinate. Could any of them compare even in that with old Stonewall? If he'd been there we would still have Vicksburg.

JAMES: Well, the butcher simply wouldn't give up, he tried four ways of getting around Vicksburg and on the fifth try he got around. Anyone else would have pulled north and—

KELLER: He wouldn't have got around if we'd had a Southerner in command, instead of a half-breed Yankee traitor like Pemberton—

(While this background talk is in progress, HELEN *is working around the table, ultimately toward* ANNIE'S *plate. She messes with her hands in* JAMES'S *plate, then in* KELLER'S, *both men taking it so for granted they hardly notice. Then* HELEN *comes groping with soiled hands past her own plate, to* ANNIE'S; *her hand goes to it, and* ANNIE, *who has been waiting, deliberately lifts and removes her hand.* HELEN *gropes again,* ANNIE *firmly pins her by the wrist, and removes her hand from the table.* HELEN *thrusts her hands again,* ANNIE *catches them, and* HELEN *begins to flail and make noises; the interruption brings* KELLER'S *gaze upon them.)*

What's the matter there?

KATE: Miss Annie. You see, she's accustomed to helping herself from our plates to anything she—

ANNIE [EVENLY]: Yes, but *I'm* not accustomed to it.

KELLER: No, of course not. Viney!

KATE: Give her something, Jimmie, to quiet her.

JAMES [BLANDLY]: But her table manners are the best she has. Well.

(He pokes across with a chunk of bacon at HELEN'S *hand, which* ANNIE *releases; but* HELEN *knocks the bacon away and stubbornly thrusts at* ANNIE'S *plate,* ANNIE *grips her wrists again, the struggle mounts.)*

KELLER: Let her this time, Miss Sullivan, it's the only way we get any adult conversation. If my son's half merits that description.

(He rises.)

I'll get you another plate.

ANNIE [GRIPPING HELEN]: I have a plate, thank you.

KATE [CALLING]: Viney! I'm afraid what Captain Keller says is only too true, she'll persist in this until she gets her own way.

KELLER [AT THE DOOR]: Viney, bring Miss Sullivan another plate—

ANNIE [STONILY]: I have a plate, nothing's wrong with the *plate*, I intend to keep it.

(Silence for a moment, except for HELEN'S *noises as she struggles to get loose; the* KELLERS *are a bit nonplussed, and* ANNIE *is too darkly intent on* HELEN'S *manners to have any thoughts now of her own.)*

JAMES: Ha. You see why they took Vicksburg?

KELLER [UNCERTAINLY]: Miss Sullivan. One plate or another is hardly a matter to struggle with a deprived child about.

ANNIE: Oh, I'd sooner have a more—

*(*HELEN *begins to kick,* ANNIE *moves her ankles to the opposite side of the chair.)*

—heroic issue myself, I—

KELLER: No, I really must insist you—

*(*HELEN *bangs her toe on the chair and sinks to the floor, crying with rage and feigned injury;* ANNIE *keeps hold of her wrists, gazing down, while* KATE *rises.)*

Now she's hurt herself.

ANNIE [GRIMLY]: No, she hasn't.

KELLER: Will you please let her hands go?

KATE: Miss Annie, you don't know the child well enough yet, she'll keep—

ANNIE: I know an ordinary tantrum well enough, when I see one, and a badly spoiled child—

JAMES: Hear, hear.

KELLER [VERY ANNOYED]: Miss Sullivan! You would have more understanding of your pupil if you had some pity in you. Now kindly do as I—

ANNIE: Pity?

(She releases HELEN to turn equally annoyed on KELLER across the table; instantly HELEN scrambles up and dives at ANNIE'S plate. This time ANNIE intercepts her by pouncing on her wrists like a hawk, and her temper boils.)

For this *tyrant?* The whole house turns on her whims, is there anything she wants she doesn't get? I'll tell you what I pity, that the sun won't rise and set for her all her life, and every day you're telling her it will, what good will your pity do her when you're under the strawberries, Captain Keller?

KELLER [OUTRAGED]: Kate, for the love of heaven will you—

KATE: Miss Annie, please, I don't think it serves to lose our—

ANNIE: It does you good, that's all. It's less trouble to feel sorry for her than to teach her anything better, isn't it?

KELLER: I fail to see where you have taught her anything yet, Miss Sullivan!

ANNIE: I'll begin this minute, if you'll leave the room, Captain Keller!

KELLER [ASTONISHED]: Leave the—

ANNIE: Everyone, please.

(She struggles with HELEN, *while* KELLER *endeavors to control his voice.)*

KELLER: Miss Sullivan, you are here only as a paid teacher. Nothing more, and not to lecture—

ANNIE: I can't *un*teach her six years of pity if you can't stand up to one tantrum! Old Stonewall, indeed. Mrs. Keller, you promised me help.

KATE: Indeed I did, we truly want to—

ANNIE: Then leave me alone with her. Now!

KELLER [IN A WRATH]: Katie, will you come outside with me? At once, please.

(He marches to the front door. KATE *and* JAMES *follow him. Simultaneously* ANNIE *releases* HELEN'S *wrists, and the child again sinks to the floor, kicking and crying her weird noises;* ANNIE *steps over her to meet* VINEY *coming in the rear doorway with biscuits and a clean plate, surprised at the general commotion.)*

VINEY: Heaven sakes—

ANNIE: Out, please.

(She backs VINEY *out with one hand, closes the door on her astonished mouth, locks it, and removes the key.* KELLER *meanwhile snatches his hat from a rack, and* KATE *follows him down the porch steps.* JAMES *lingers in the doorway to address* ANNIE *across the room with a bow.)*

JAMES: If it takes all summer, general.

*(*ANNIE *comes over to his door in turn, removing her glasses grimly; as* KELLER *outside begins speaking,* ANNIE *closes the door on* JAMES, *locks it, removes the key, and turns with her back against the door to stare ominously at* HELEN, *kicking on the floor.)*

JAMES *takes his hat from the rack, and going down the porch steps joins* KATE *and* KELLER *talking in the yard,* KELLER *in a sputter of ire.)*

KELLER: This girl, this—cub of a girl—*presumes!* I tell you, I'm of half a mind to ship her back to Boston before the week is out. You can inform her so from me!

KATE [EYEBROWS UP]: I, Captain?

KELLER: She's a *hireling!* Now I want it clear, unless there's an apology and complete change of manner she goes back on the next train! Will you make that quite clear?

KATE: Where will you be, Captain, while I am making it quite—

KELLER: At the office!

(He begins off left, finds his napkin still in his irate hand, is uncertain with it, dabs his lips with dignity, gets rid of it in a toss to JAMES, *and marches off.* JAMES *turns to eye* KATE.)*

JAMES: Will you?

*(*KATE'S *mouth is set, and* JAMES *studies it lightly.)*

I thought what she said was exceptionally intelligent. I've been saying it for years.

KATE [NOT WITHOUT SCORN]: To his face?

(She comes to relieve him of the white napkin, but reverts again with it.)

Or will you take it, Jimmie? As a flag?

*(*JAMES *stalks out, much offended, and* KATE *turning stares across the yard at the house; the lights narrowing down to the following pantomime in the family room leave her motionless in the dark.*

ANNIE *meanwhile has begun by slapping both keys down on a shelf out of* HELEN'S *reach; she returns to the table, upstage.*

HELEN'S *kicking has subsided, and when from the floor her hand finds* ANNIE'S *chair empty she pauses.* ANNIE *clears the table of* KATE'S, JAMES'S, *and* KELLER'S *plates; she gets back to her own across the table just in time to slide it deftly away from* HELEN'S *pouncing hand. She lifts the hand and moves it to* HELEN'S *plate, and after an instant's exploration,* HELEN *sits again on the floor and drums her heels.* ANNIE *comes around the table and resumes her chair. When* HELEN *feels her skirt again, she ceases kicking, waits for whatever is to come, renews some kicking, waits again.* ANNIE *retrieving her plate takes up a forkful of food, stops it halfway to her mouth, gazes at it devoid of appetite, and half-lowers it; but after a look at* HELEN *she sighs, dips the forkful toward* HELEN *in a for-your-sake toast, and puts it in her own mouth to chew, not without an effort.*

HELEN *now gets hold of the chair leg, and half-succeeds in pulling the chair out from under her.* ANNIE *bangs it down with her rear, heavily, and sits with all her weight.* HELEN'S *next attempt to topple it is unavailing, so her fingers dive in a pinch at* ANNIE'S *flank.* ANNIE *in the middle of her mouthful almost loses it with startle, and she slaps down her fork to round on* HELEN. *The child comes up with curiosity to feel what* ANNIE *is doing, so* ANNIE *resumes eating, letting* HELEN'S *hand follow the movement of her fork to her mouth; whereupon* HELEN *at once reaches into* ANNIE'S *plate.* ANNIE *firmly removes her hand to her own plate.* HELEN *in reply pinches* ANNIE'S *thigh, a good mean pinchful that makes* ANNIE *jump.* ANNIE *sets the fork down, and sits with her mouth tight.* HELEN *digs another pinch into her thigh, and this time* ANNIE *slaps her hand smartly away;* HELEN *retaliates with a roundhouse fist that catches* ANNIE *on the ear, and* ANNIE'S *hand leaps at once in a forceful slap across* HELEN'S *cheek;* HELEN *is the startled one now.* ANNIE'S *hand in compunction falters to her own face, but when* HELEN *hits at her again,* ANNIE *deliberately slaps her again.* HELEN *lifts her fist irresolute for another roundhouse,* ANNIE *lifts her hand resolute for another slap, and they freeze in this posture, while* HELEN *mulls it over. She thinks better of it, drops her fist, and giving* ANNIE *a wide berth, gropes around to her* MOTHER'S *chair, to find it empty; she blunders her way along the table upstage, and encountering the empty chairs and missing plates, she looks bewildered; she gropes back to her* MOTHER'S *chair,*

*again touches her cheek and indicates the chair, and waits for
the world to answer.*

ANNIE *now reaches over to spell into her hand, but* HELEN *yanks
it away; she gropes to the front door, tries the knob, and finds
the door locked, with no key. She gropes to the rear door, and
finds it locked, with no key. She commences to bang on it.* ANNIE
*rises, crosses, takes her wrists, draws her resisting back to the
table, seats her, and releases her hands upon her plate; as* ANNIE
herself begins to sit, HELEN *writhes out of her chair, runs to the
front door, and tugs and kicks at it.* ANNIE *rises again, crosses,
draws her by one wrist back to the table, seats her, and sits;*
HELEN *escapes back to the door, knocking over her* MOTHER'S
chair en route. ANNIE *rises again in pursuit, and this time lifts*
HELEN *bodily from behind and bears her kicking to her chair.
She deposits her, and once more turns to sit.* HELEN *scrambles
out, but as she passes* ANNIE *catches her up again from behind
and deposits her in the chair;* HELEN *scrambles out on the other
side, for the rear door, but* ANNIE *at her heels catches her up and
deposits her again in the chair. She stands behind it.* HELEN
scrambles out to her right, and the instant her feet hit the floor
ANNIE *lifts and deposits her back; she scrambles out to her left,
and is at once lifted and deposited back. She tries right again
and is deposited back, and tries left again and is deposited back,
and now feints* ANNIE *to the right but is off to her left, and is
promptly deposited back. She sits a moment, and then starts
straight over the tabletop, dishware notwithstanding;* ANNIE
*hauls her in and deposits her back, with her plate spilling in her
lap, and she melts to the floor and crawls under the table, labori-
ous among its legs and chairs; but* ANNIE *is swift around the
table and waiting on the other side when she surfaces, immedi-
ately bearing her aloft;* HELEN *clutches at* JAMES'S *chair for
anchorage, but it comes with her, and halfway back she aban-
dons it to the floor.* ANNIE *deposits her in her chair, and waits.*
HELEN *sits tensed motionless. Then she tentatively puts out her
left foot and hand,* ANNIE *interposes her own hand, and at the
contact* HELEN *jerks hers in. She tries her right foot,* ANNIE
blocks it with her own, and HELEN *jerks hers in. Finally, leaning
back, she slumps down in her chair, in a sullen biding.*

ANNIE *backs off a step, and watches;* HELEN *offers no move.*
ANNIE *takes a deep breath. Both of them and the room are in
considerable disorder, two chairs down and the table a mess, but*
ANNIE *makes no effort to tidy it; she only sits on her own chair,
and lets her energy refill. Then she takes up knife and fork, and
resolutely addresses her food.* HELEN'S *hand comes out to explore, and seeing it* ANNIE *sits without moving; the child's hand
goes over her hand and fork, pauses—*ANNIE *still does not move
—and withdraws. Presently it moves for her own plate, slaps
about for it, and stops, thwarted. At this,* ANNIE *again rises,
recovers* HELEN'S *plate from the floor and a handful of scattered
food from the deranged tablecloth, drops it on the plate, and
pushes the plate into contact with* HELEN'S *fist. Neither of them
now moves for a pregnant moment—until* HELEN *suddenly
takes a grab of food and wolfs it down.* ANNIE *permits herself
the humor of a minor bow and warming of her hands together;
she wanders off a step or two, watching.* HELEN *cleans up the
plate.*

*After a glower of indecision, she holds the empty plate out for
more.* ANNIE *accepts it, and crossing to the removed plates,
spoons food from them onto it; she stands debating the spoon,
tapping it a few times on* HELEN'S *plate; and when she returns
with the plate she brings the spoon, too. She puts the spoon first
into* HELEN'S *hand, then sets the plate down.* HELEN *discarding
the spoon reaches with her hand, and* ANNIE *stops it by the
wrist; she replaces the spoon in it.* HELEN *impatiently discards it
again, and again* ANNIE *stops her hand, to replace the spoon in
it. This time* HELEN *throws the spoon on the floor.* ANNIE *after
considering it lifts* HELEN *bodily out of the chair, and in a
wrestling match on the floor closes her fingers upon the spoon,
and returns her with it to the chair.* HELEN *again throws the
spoon on the floor.* ANNIE *lifts her out of the chair again; but in
the struggle over the spoon* HELEN *with* ANNIE *on her back sends
her sliding over her head;* HELEN *flees back to her chair and
scrambles into it. When* ANNIE *comes after her she clutches it for
dear life;* ANNIE *pries one hand loose, then the other, then the
first again, then the other again, and then lifts* HELEN *by the
waist, chair and all, and shakes the chair loose.* HELEN *wrestles
to get free, but* ANNIE *pins her to the floor, closes her fingers
upon the spoon, and lifts her kicking under one arm; with her*

other hand she gets the chair in place again, and plunks HELEN
back on it. When she releases her hand, HELEN *throws the spoon
at her.*

ANNIE *now removes the plate of food.* HELEN *grabbing finds it
missing, and commences to bang with her fists on the table.*
ANNIE *collects a fistful of spoons and descends with them and
the plate on* HELEN; *she lets her smell the plate, at which* HELEN
ceases banging, and ANNIE *puts the plate down and a spoon in*
HELEN'S *hand.* HELEN *throws it on the floor.* ANNIE *puts another
spoon in her hand.* HELEN *throws it on the floor.* ANNIE *puts
another spoon in her hand.* HELEN *throws it on the floor. When*
ANNIE *comes to her last spoon she sits next to* HELEN, *and grip-
ping the spoon in* HELEN'S *hand compels her to take food in it
up to her mouth.* HELEN *sits with lips shut.* ANNIE *waits a stolid
moment, then lowers* HELEN'S *hand. She tries again;* HELEN'S
lips remain shut. ANNIE *waits, lowers* HELEN'S *hand. She tries
again; this time* HELEN *suddenly opens her mouth and accepts
the food.* ANNIE *lowers the spoon with a sigh of relief, and*
HELEN *spews the mouthful out at her face.* ANNIE *sits a moment
with eyes closed, then takes the pitcher and dashes its water into*
HELEN'S *face, who gasps astonished.* ANNIE *with* HELEN'S *hand
takes up another spoonful, and shoves it into her open mouth.*
HELEN *swallows involuntarily, and while she is catching her
breath* ANNIE *forces her palm open, throws four swift letters
into it, then another four, and bows toward her with devastating
pleasantness.)*

ANNIE: Good girl.

*(*ANNIE *lifts* HELEN'S *hand to feel her face nodding;* HELEN
grabs a fistful of her hair, and yanks. The pain brings ANNIE *to
her knees, and* HELEN *pummels her; they roll under the table,
and the lights commence to dim out on them.*

*Simultaneously the light at left has been rising, slowly, so
slowly that it seems at first we only imagine what is intimated in
the yard: a few ghostlike figures, in silence, motionless, waiting.
Now the distant belfry chimes commence to toll the hour, also
very slowly, almost—it is twelve—interminably; the sense is
that of a long time passing. We can identify the figures before*

the twelfth stroke, all facing the house in a kind of watch: KATE
is standing exactly as before, but now with the baby MILDRED
sleeping in her arms, and placed here and there, unmoving, are
AUNT EV *in her hat with a hanky to her nose, and the two Negro
children,* PERCY *and* MARTHA *with necks outstretched eagerly,
and* VINEY *with a knotted kerchief on her head and a feather
duster in her hand.*

*The chimes cease, and there is silence. For a long moment none
of the group moves.)*

VINEY [PRESENTLY]: What am I gone do, Miss Kate? It's noontime,
dinner's comin', I didn't get them breakfast dishes out of there
yet.

*(*KATE *says nothing, stares at the house.* MARTHA *shifts* HELEN'S
doll in her clutch, and it plaintively says momma.)

KATE [PRESENTLY]: You run along, Martha.

*(*AUNT EV *blows her nose.)*

AUNT EV [WRETCHEDLY]: I can't wait out here a minute longer,
Kate, why, this could go on all afternoon, too.

KATE: I'll tell the captain you called.

VINEY [TO THE CHILDREN]: You hear what Miss Kate say? Never
you mind what's going on here.

(Still no one moves.)

You run along tend your own bizness.

(Finally VINEY *turns on the children with the feather duster.)*

Shoo!

(The two children divide before her. She chases them off. AUNT
EV *comes to* KATE, *on her dignity.)*

AUNT EV: Say what you like, Kate, but that child is a *Keller.*

(She opens her parasol, preparatory to leaving.)

I needn't remind you that all the Kellers are cousins to General Robert E. Lee. I don't know *who* that girl is.

(She waits; but KATE *staring at the house is without response.)*

The only Sullivan I've heard of—from Boston too, and I'd think twice before locking her up with that kind—is that man John L.

(And AUNT EV *departs, with head high. Presently* VINEY *comes to* KATE, *her arms out for the baby.)*

VINEY: You give me her, Miss Kate, I'll sneak her in back, to her crib.

(But KATE *is moveless, until* VINEY *starts to take the baby;* KATE *looks down at her before relinquishing her.)*

KATE [SLOWLY]: This child never gives me a minute's worry.

VINEY: Oh yes, this one's the angel of the family, no question bout *that.*

(She begins off rear with the baby, heading around the house; and KATE *now turns her back on it, her hand to her eyes. At this moment there is the slamming of a door, and when* KATE *wheels* HELEN *is blundering down the porch steps into the light, like a ruined bat out of hell.* VINEY *halts, and* KATE *runs in;* HELEN *collides with her mother's knees, and reels off and back to clutch them as her savior.* ANNIE *with smoked glasses in hand stands on the porch, also much undone, looking as though she had indeed just taken Vicksburg.* KATE *taking in* HELEN'S *ravaged state becomes steely in her gaze up at* ANNIE.)*

KATE: What happened?

*(ANNIE *meets* KATE'S *gaze, and gives a factual report, too exhausted for anything but a flat voice.)*

ANNIE: She ate from her own plate.

(She thinks a moment.)

She ate with a spoon. Herself.

(KATE *frowns, uncertain with thought, and glances down at* HELEN.)

And she folded her napkin.

(KATE'S *gaze now wavers, from* HELEN *to* ANNIE, *and back.)*

KATE [SOFTLY]: Folded—her napkin?

ANNIE: The room's a wreck, but her napkin is folded.

(She pauses, then:)

I'll be in my room, Mrs. Keller.

(She moves to re-enter the house; but she stops at VINEY'S *voice.)*

VINEY [CHEERY]: Don't be long, Miss Annie. Dinner be ready right away!

(VINEY *carries* MILDRED *around the back of the house.* ANNIE *stands unmoving, takes a deep breath, stares over her shoulder at* KATE *and* HELEN, *then inclines her head graciously, and goes with a slight stagger into the house. The lights in her room above steal up in readiness for her.*

KATE *remains alone with* HELEN *in the yard, standing protectively over her, in a kind of wonder.)*

KATE [SLOWLY]: Folded her napkin.

(She contemplates the wild head in her thighs, and moves her fingertips over it, with such a tenderness, and something like a fear of its strangeness, that her own eyes close; she whispers, bending to it:)

My Helen—folded her napkin—

(And still erect, with only her head in surrender, KATE *for the first time that we see loses her protracted war with grief; but she will not let a sound escape her, only the grimace of tears comes, and sobs that shake her in a grip of silence. But* HELEN *feels them, and her hand comes up in its own wondering, to interrogate her mother's face, until* KATE *buries her lips in the child's palm.*

Upstairs, ANNIE *enters her room, closes the door, and stands back against it; the lights, growing on her with their special color, commence to fade on* KATE *and* HELEN. *Then* ANNIE *goes wearily to her suitcase, and lifts it to take it toward the bed. But it knocks an object to the floor, and she turns back to regard it. A new voice comes in a cultured murmur, hesitant as with the effort of remembering a text:)*

MAN'S VOICE: This—soul—

*(*ANNIE *puts the suitcase down, and kneels to the object: it is the battered Perkins report, and she stands with it in her hand, letting memory try to speak:)*

This—blind, deaf, mute—woman—

*(*ANNIE *sits on her bed, opens the book, and finding the passage, brings it up an inch from her eyes to read, her face and lips following the overheard words, the voice quite factual now:)*

Can nothing be done to disinter this human soul? The whole neighborhood would rush to save this woman if she were buried alive by the caving in of a pit, and labor with zeal until she were dug out. Now if there were one who had as much patience as zeal, he might awaken her to a consciousness of her immortal—

(When the boy's voice comes, ANNIE *closes her eyes, in pain.)*

BOY'S VOICE: Annie? Annie, you there?

ANNIE: Hush.

BOY'S VOICE: Annie, what's that noise?

(ANNIE *tries not to answer; her own voice is drawn out of her, unwilling.*)

ANNIE: Just a cot, Jimmie.

BOY'S VOICE: Where they pushin' it?

ANNIE: To the deadhouse.

BOY'S VOICE: Annie. Does it hurt, to be dead?

(ANNIE *escapes by opening her eyes, her hand works restlessly over her cheek; she retreats into the book again, but the cracked old crones interrupt, whispering.* ANNIE *slowly lowers the book.*)

FIRST CRONE'S VOICE: There is schools.

SECOND CRONE'S VOICE: There is schools outside—

THIRD CRONE'S VOICE: —schools where they teach blind ones, worse'n you—

FIRST CRONE'S VOICE: To read—

SECOND CRONE'S VOICE: To read and write—

THIRD CRONE'S VOICE: There is schools outside where they—

FIRST CRONE'S VOICE: There is schools—

(*Silence.* ANNIE *sits with her eyes shining, her hand almost in a caress over the book. Then:*)

BOY'S VOICE: You ain't goin' to school, are you, Annie?

ANNIE [WHISPERING]: When I grow up.

BOY'S VOICE: You ain't either, Annie. You're goin' to stay here take care of me.

ANNIE: I'm goin' to school when I grow up.

BOY'S VOICE: You said we'll be together, forever and ever and ever—

ANNIE [FIERCE]: I'm goin' to school when I grow up!

DOCTOR'S VOICE [SLOWLY]: Little girl. Little girl, I must tell you. Your brother will be going on a journey, soon.

(ANNIE *sits rigid, in silence. Then the boy's voice pierces it, a shriek of terror.*)

BOY'S VOICE: *Annie!*

(*It goes into* ANNIE *like a sword, she doubles onto it; the book falls to the floor. It takes her a racked moment to find herself and what she was engaged in here; when she sees the suitcase she remembers, and lifts it once again toward the bed. But the voices are with her, as she halts with suitcase in hand.*)

FIRST CRONE'S VOICE: Goodbye, Annie.

DOCTOR'S VOICE: Write me when you learn how.

SECOND CRONE'S VOICE: Don't tell anyone you came from here. Don't tell anyone—

THIRD CRONE'S VOICE: Yeah, don't tell anyone you came from—

FIRST CRONE'S VOICE: Yeah, don't tell anyone—

SECOND CRONE'S VOICE: Don't tell any—

(*The echoing voices fade. After a moment* ANNIE *lays the suitcase on the bed; and the last voice comes faintly, from far away.*)

BOY'S VOICE: Annie. It hurts, to be dead. Forever.

(ANNIE *falls to her knees by the bed, stifling her mouth in it. When at last she rolls blindly away from it, her palm comes down on the open report; she opens her eyes, regards it dully, and then, still on her knees, takes in the print.*)

MAN'S VOICE [FACTUAL]: —might awaken her to a consciousness of her immortal nature. The chance is small indeed; but with a smaller chance they would have dug desperately for her in the pit; and is the life of the soul of less import than that of the body?

(ANNIE *gets to her feet. She drops the book on the bed, and pauses over her suitcase; after a moment she unclasps and opens it. Standing before it, she comes to her decision; she at once turns to the bureau, and taking her things out of its drawers, commences to throw them into the open suitcase.*

In the darkness down left a hand strikes a match, and lights a hanging oil lamp. It is KELLER'S *hand, and his voice accompanies it, very angry; the lights rising here before they fade on* ANNIE *show* KELLER *and* KATE *inside a suggestion of a garden house, with a bay-window seat towards center and a door at back.)*

KELLER: Kate, I will not *have* it! Now you did not see when that girl after supper tonight went to look for Helen in her room—

KATE: No.

KELLER: The child practically climbed out of her window to escape from her! What kind of teacher *is* she? I thought I had seen her at her worst this morning, shouting at me, but I come home to find the entire house disorganized by her—Helen won't stay one second in the same room, won't come to the table with her, won't let herself be bathed or undressed or put to bed by her, or even by Viney now, and the end result is that *you* have to do more for the child than before we hired this girl's services! From the moment she stepped off the train she's been nothing but a burden, incompetent, impertinent, ineffectual, immodest—

KATE: She folded her napkin, Captain.

KELLER: What?

KATE: Not ineffectual. Helen did fold her napkin.

KELLER: What in heaven's name is so extraordinary about folding a napkin?

KATE [WITH SOME HUMOR]: Well. It's more than you did, Captain.

KELLER: Katie. I did not bring you all the way out here to the garden house to be frivolous. Now, how does Miss Sullivan propose to teach a deaf-blind pupil who won't let her even touch her?

KATE [A PAUSE]: I don't know.

KELLER: The fact is, today she scuttled any chance she ever had of getting along with the child. If you can see any point or purpose to her staying on here longer, it's more than—

KATE: What do you wish me to do?

KELLER: I want you to give her notice.

KATE: I can't.

KELLER: Then if you won't, I must. I simply will not—

(He is interrupted by a knock at the back door. KELLER after a glance at KATE moves to open the door; ANNIE in her smoked glasses is standing outside. KELLER contemplates her, heavily.)

Miss Sullivan.

ANNIE: Captain Keller.

(She is nervous, keyed up to seizing the bull by the horns again, and she assumes a cheeriness which is not unshaky.)

Viney said I'd find you both over here in the garden house. I thought we should—have a talk?

KELLER [RELUCTANTLY]: Yes, I— Well, come in.

(ANNIE enters, and is interested in this room; she rounds on her heel, anxiously, studying it. KELLER turns the matter over to KATE, sotto voce.)

Katie.

KATE [TURNING IT BACK, COURTEOUSLY]: Captain.

(KELLER clears his throat, makes ready.)

KELLER: I, ah—wanted first to make my position clear to Mrs. Keller, in private. I have decided I—am not satisfied—in fact, am deeply dissatisfied—with the manner in which—

ANNIE [INTENT]: Excuse me, is this little house ever in use?

KELLER [WITH PATIENCE]: In the hunting season. If you will give me your attention, Miss Sullivan.

(ANNIE *turns her smoked glasses upon him; they hold his unwilling stare.*)

I have tried to make allowances for you because you come from a part of the country where people are—women, I should say—come from who—well, for whom—

(*It begins to elude him.*)

—allowances must—be made. I have decided, nevertheless, to—that is, decided I—

(*Vexedly*)

Miss Sullivan, I find it difficult to talk through those glasses.

ANNIE [EAGERLY, REMOVING THEM]: Oh, of course.

KELLER [DOURLY]: Why do you wear them, the sun has been down for an hour.

ANNIE [PLEASANTLY, AT THE LAMP]: Any kind of light hurts my eyes.

(*A silence;* KELLER *ponders her, heavily.*)

KELLER: Put them on. Miss Sullivan, I have decided to—give you another chance.

ANNIE [CHEERFULLY]: To do what?

KELLER: To—remain in our employ.

(ANNIE'S *eyes widen.*)

But on two conditions. I am not accustomed to rudeness in servants or women, and that is the first. If you are to stay, there must be a radical change of manner.

ANNIE [A PAUSE]: Whose?

KELLER [EXPLODING]: Yours, young lady, isn't it obvious? And the second is that you persuade me there's the slightest hope of your teaching a child who flees from you now like the plague, to anyone else she can find in this house.

ANNIE [A PAUSE]: There isn't.

(KATE *stops sewing, and fixes her eyes upon* ANNIE.)

KATE: What, Miss Annie?

ANNIE: It's hopeless here. I can't teach a child who runs away.

KELLER [NONPLUSSED]: Then—do I understand you—propose—

ANNIE: Well, if we all agree it's hopeless, the next question is what—

KATE: Miss Annie.

(*She is leaning toward* ANNIE, *in deadly earnest; it commands both* ANNIE *and* KELLER.)

I am not agreed. I think perhaps you—underestimate Helen.

ANNIE: I think everybody else here does.

KATE: She did fold her napkin. She learns, she learns, do you know she began talking when she was six months old? She could say "water." Not really—"wahwah." "Wahwah," but she meant water, she knew what it meant, and only six months old, I never saw a child so—bright, or outgoing—

(*Her voice is unsteady, but she gets it level.*)

It's still in her, somewhere, isn't it? You should have seen her before her illness, such a good-tempered child—

ANNIE [AGREEABLY]: She's changed.

(*A pause,* KATE *not letting her eyes go; her appeal at last is unconditional, and very quiet.*)

KATE: Miss Annie, put up with it. And with us.

KELLER: Us!

KATE: Please? Like the lost lamb in the parable, I love her all the more.

ANNIE: Mrs. Keller, I don't think Helen's worst handicap is deafness or blindness. I think it's your love. And pity.

KELLER: Now what does that mean?

ANNIE: All of you here are so sorry for her you've kept her—like a pet, why, even a dog you housebreak. No wonder she won't let me come near her. It's useless for me to try to teach her language or anything else here. I might as well—

KATE [CUTS IN]: Miss Annie, before you came we spoke of putting her in an asylum.

(ANNIE *turns back to regard her. A pause.*)

ANNIE: What kind of asylum?

KELLER: For mental defectives.

KATE: I visited there. I can't tell you what I saw, people like—animals, with—*rats,* in the halls, and—

(*She shakes her head on her vision.*)

What else are we to do, if you give up?

ANNIE: Give up?

KATE: You said it was hopeless.

ANNIE: Here. Give up, why, I only today saw what has to be done, to begin!

(*She glances from* KATE *to* KELLER, *who stare, waiting; and she makes it as plain and simple as her nervousness permits.*)

I—want complete charge of her.

KELLER: You already have that. It has resulted in—

ANNIE: No, I mean day and night. She has to be dependent on me.

KATE: For what?

ANNIE: Everything. The food she eats, the clothes she wears, fresh—

(She is amused at herself, though very serious.)

—air, yes, the air she breathes, whatever her body needs is a— primer, to teach her out of. It's the only way, the one who lets her have it should be her teacher.

(She considers them in turn; they digest it, KELLER *frowning,* KATE *perplexed.)*

Not anyone who *loves* her, you have so many feelings they fall over each other like feet, you won't use your chances and you won't let me.

KATE: But if she runs from you—*to* us—

ANNIE: Yes, that's the point. I'll have to live with her somewhere else.

KELLER: What!

ANNIE: Till she learns to depend on and listen to me.

KATE [NOT WITHOUT ALARM]: For how long?

ANNIE: As long as it takes.

(A pause. She takes a breath.)

I packed half my things already.

KELLER: Miss—Sullivan!

(But when ANNIE *attends upon him he is speechless, and she is merely earnest.)*

ANNIE: Captain Keller, it meets both your conditions. It's the one way I can get back in touch with Helen, and I don't see how I can be rude to you again if you're not around to interfere with me.

KELLER [RED-FACED]: And what is your intention if I say no? Pack the other half, for home, and abandon your charge to—to—

ANNIE: The asylum?

(She waits, appraises KELLER'S *glare and* KATE'S *uncertainty, and decides to use her weapons.)*

I grew up in such an asylum. The state almshouse.

*(*KATE'S *head comes up on this, and* KELLER *stares hard;* ANNIE'S *tone is cheerful enough, albeit level as gunfire.)*

Rats—why, my brother Jimmie and I used to play with the rats because we didn't have toys. Maybe you'd like to know what Helen will find there, not on visiting days? One ward was full of the—old women, crippled, blind, most of them dying, but even if what they had was catching there was nowhere else to move them, and that's where they put us. There were younger ones across the hall, prostitutes mostly, with T.B., and epileptic fits, and a couple of the kind who—keep after other girls, especially young ones, and some insane. Some just had the D.T.'s. The youngest were in another ward to have babies they didn't want, they started at thirteen, fourteen. They'd leave afterwards, but the babies stayed and we played with them, too, though a lot of them had—sores all over from diseases you're not supposed to talk about, but not many of them lived. The first year we had eighty, seventy died. The room Jimmie and I played in was the deadhouse, where they kept the bodies till they could dig—

KATE [CLOSES HER EYES]: Oh, my dear—

ANNIE: —the graves.

(She is immune to KATE'S *compassion.)*

No, it made me strong. But I don't think you need send Helen there. She's strong enough.

(She waits again; but when neither offers her a word, she simply concludes.)

No, I have no conditions, Captain Keller.

KATE [NOT LOOKING UP]: Miss Annie.

ANNIE: Yes.

KATE [A PAUSE]: Where would you—take Helen?

ANNIE: Ohh—

(Brightly)

Italy?

KELLER [WHEELING]: What?

ANNIE: Can't have everything, how would this garden house do? Furnish it, bring Helen here after a long ride so she won't recognize it, and you can see her every day. If she doesn't know. Well?

KATE [A SIGH OF RELIEF]: Is that all?

ANNIE: That's all.

KATE: Captain.

(KELLER turns his head; and KATE's request is quiet but firm.)

With your permission?

KELLER [TEETH IN CIGAR]: Why must she depend on you for the food she eats?

ANNIE [A PAUSE]: I want control of it.

KELLER: Why?

ANNIE: It's a way to reach her.

KELLER [STARES]: You intend to *starve* her into letting you touch her?

ANNIE: She won't starve, she'll learn. All's fair in love and war, Captain Keller, you never cut supplies?

KELLER: This is hardly a war!

ANNIE: Well, it's not love. A siege is a siege.

KELLER [HEAVILY]: Miss Sullivan. Do you *like* the child?

ANNIE [STRAIGHT IN HIS EYES]: Do you?

(A long pause.)

KATE: You could have a servant here—

ANNIE [AMUSED]: I'll have enough work without looking after a servant! But that boy Percy could sleep here, run errands—

KATE [ALSO AMUSED]: We can let Percy sleep here, I think, Captain?

ANNIE [EAGERLY]: And some old furniture, all our own—

KATE [ALSO EAGER]: Captain? Do you think that walnut bedstead in the barn would be too—

KELLER: I have not yet consented to Percy! Or to the house, or to the proposal! Or to Miss Sullivan's—staying on when I—

(But he erupts in an irate surrender.)

Very well, I consent to everything!

(He shakes the cigar at ANNIE.*)*

For two weeks. I'll give you two weeks in this place, and it will be a miracle if you get the child to tolerate you.

KATE: Two weeks? Miss Annie, can you accomplish anything in two weeks?

KELLER: Anything or not, two weeks, then the child comes back to us. Make up your mind, Miss Sullivan, yes or no?

ANNIE: Two weeks. For only one miracle?

(She nods at him, nervously.)

I'll get her to tolerate me.

*(*KELLER *marches out, and slams the door.* KATE *on her feet regards* ANNIE, *who is facing the door.)*

KATE [THEN]: You can't think as little of love as you said.

*(*ANNIE *glances questioning.)*

Or you wouldn't stay.

ANNIE [A PAUSE]: I didn't come here for love. I came for money!

(KATE *shakes her head to this, with a smile; after a moment she extends her open hand.* ANNIE *looks at it, but when she puts hers out it is not to shake hands, it is to set her fist in* KATE'S *palm.*)

KATE [PUZZLED]: Hm?

ANNIE: A. It's the first of many. Twenty-six!

(KATE *squeezes her fist, squeezes it hard, and hastens out after* KELLER. ANNIE *stands as the door closes behind her, her manner so apprehensive that finally she slaps her brow, holds it, sighs, and, with her eyes closed, crosses herself for luck.*

The lights dim into a cool silhouette scene around her, the lamp paling out, and now, in formal entrances, persons appear around ANNIE *with furniture for the room:* PERCY *crosses the stage with a rocking chair and waits;* MARTHA *from another direction bears in a stool,* VINEY *bears in a small table, and the other Negro servant rolls in a bed partway from left; and* ANNIE, *opening her eyes to put her glasses back on, sees them. She turns around in the room once, and goes into action, pointing out locations for each article; the servants place them and leave, and* ANNIE *then darts around, interchanging them. In the midst of this—while* PERCY *and* MARTHA *reappear with a tray of food and a chair, respectively—*JAMES *comes down from the house with* ANNIE'S *suitcase, and stands viewing the room and her quizzically;* ANNIE *halts abruptly under his eyes, embarrassed, then seizes the suitcase from his hand, explaining herself brightly.*)

ANNIE: I always wanted to live in a doll's house!

(*She sets the suitcase out of the way, and continues;* VINEY *at left appears to position a rod with drapes for a doorway, and the other servant at center pushes in a wheelbarrow loaded with a couple of boxes of* HELEN'S *toys and clothes.* ANNIE *helps lift them into the room, and the servant pushes the wheelbarrow off. In none of this is any heed taken of the imaginary walls of the garden house, the furniture is moved in from every side and itself defines the walls.*

ANNIE *now drags the box of toys into center, props up the doll conspicuously on top; with the people melted away, except for* JAMES, *all is again still. The lights turn again without pause, rising warmer.)*

JAMES: You don't let go of things easily, do you? How will you— win her hand now, in this place?

ANNIE [CURTLY]: Do I know? I lost my temper, and here we are!

JAMES [LIGHTLY]: No touching, no teaching. Of course, you *are* bigger—

ANNIE: I'm not counting on force, I'm counting on her. That little imp is dying to know.

JAMES: Know what?

ANNIE: Anything. Any and every crumb in God's creation. I'll have to use that appetite too.

(She gives the room a final survey, straightens the bed, arranges the curtains.)

JAMES [A PAUSE]: Maybe she'll teach you.

ANNIE: Of course.

JAMES: That she isn't. That there's such a thing as—dullness of heart. Acceptance. And letting go. Sooner or later we all give up, don't we?

ANNIE: Maybe you all do. It's my idea of the original sin.

JAMES: What is?

ANNIE [WITHERINGLY]: Giving up.

JAMES [NETTLED]: You won't open her. Why can't you let her be? Have some—pity on her, for being what she is—

ANNIE: If I'd ever once thought like that, I'd be dead!

JAMES [PLEASANTLY]: You will be. Why trouble?

(ANNIE *turns to glare at him; he is mocking.*)

Or will you teach me?

(*And with a bow, he drifts off.*

Now in the distance there comes the clopping of hoofs, drawing near, and nearer, up to the door; and they halt. ANNIE *wheels to face the door. When it opens this time, the* KELLERS—KATE *in travelling bonnet,* KELLER *also hatted—are standing there with* HELEN *between them; she is in a cloak.* KATE *gently cues her into the room.* HELEN *comes in groping, baffled, but interested in the new surroundings;* ANNIE *evades her exploring hand, her gaze not leaving the child.*)

ANNIE: Does she know where she is?

KATE [SHAKES HER HEAD]: We rode her out in the country for two hours.

KELLER: For all she knows, she could be in another town—

(HELEN *stumbles over the box on the floor and in it discovers her doll and other battered toys, is pleased, sits to them, then becomes puzzled and suddenly very wary. She scrambles up and back to her mother's thighs, but* ANNIE *steps in, and it is hers that* HELEN *embraces.* HELEN *recoils, gropes, and touches her cheek instantly.*)

KATE: That's her sign for me.

ANNIE: I know.

(HELEN *waits, then recommences her groping, more urgently.* KATE *stands indecisive, and takes an abrupt step toward her, but* ANNIE'S *hand is a barrier.*)

In two weeks.

KATE: Miss Annie, I— Please be good to her. These two weeks, try to be very good to her—

ANNIE: I will.

(KATE, *turning then, hurries out. The* KELLERS *cross back of the main house.*

ANNIE *closes the door.* HELEN *starts at the door jar, and rushes it.* ANNIE *holds her off.* HELEN *kicks her, breaks free, and careens around the room like an imprisoned bird, colliding with furniture, groping wildly, repeatedly touching her cheek in a growing panic. When she has covered the room, she commences her weird screaming.* ANNIE *moves to comfort her, but her touch sends* HELEN *into a paroxysm of rage: she tears away, falls over her box of toys, flings its contents in handfuls in* ANNIE'S *direction, flings the box too, reels to her feet, rips curtains from the window, bangs and kicks at the door, sweeps objects off the mantelpiece and shelf, a little tornado incarnate, all destruction, until she comes upon her doll and, in the act of hurling it, freezes. Then she clutches it to herself, and in exhaustion sinks sobbing to the floor.* ANNIE *stands contemplating her, in some awe.)*

Two weeks.

(She shakes her head, not without a touch of disgusted bewilderment.)

What did I get into now?

(The lights have been dimming throughout, and the garden house is lit only by moonlight now, with ANNIE *lost in the patches of dark.*

KATE, *now hatless and coatless, enters the family room by the rear door, carrying a lamp.* KELLER, *also hatless, wanders simultaneously around the back of the main house to where* JAMES *has been waiting, in the rising moonlight, on the porch.)*

KELLER: I can't understand it. I had every intention of dismissing that girl, not setting her up like an empress.

JAMES: Yes, what's her secret, sir?

KELLER: Secret?

JAMES [PLEASANTLY]: That enables her to get anything she wants out of you? When I can't.

(JAMES *turns to go into the house, but* KELLER *grasps his wrist, twisting him half to his knees.* KATE *comes from the porch.*)

KELLER [ANGRILY]: She does *not* get anything she—

JAMES [IN PAIN]: Don't—don't—

KATE: Captain.

KELLER: He's afraid.

(*He throws* JAMES *away from him, with contempt.*)

What *does* he want out of me?

JAMES [AN OUTCRY]: My God, don't you know?

(*He gazes from* KELLER *to* KATE.)

Everything you forgot, when you forgot my mother.

KELLER: What!

(JAMES *wheels into the house.* KELLER *takes a stride to the porch, to roar after him.*)

One thing that girl's secret is not, she doesn't fire one shot and disappear!

(KATE *stands rigid, and* KELLER *comes back to her.*)

Katie. Don't mind what he—

KATE: Captain, *I* am proud of you.

KELLER: For what?

KATE: For letting this girl have what she needs.

KELLER: Why can't my son be? He can't bear me, you'd think I treat him as hard as this girl does Helen—

(He breaks off, as it dawns in him.)

KATE [GENTLY]: Perhaps you do.

KELLER: But he has to learn some respect!

KATE [A PAUSE, WRYLY]: *Do* you like the child?

(She turns again to the porch, but pauses, reluctant.)

How empty the house is, tonight.

(After a moment she continues on in. KELLER stands moveless, as the moonlight dies on him.

The distant belfry chimes toll, two o'clock, and with them, a moment later, comes the boy's voice on the wind, in a whisper:)

BOY'S VOICE: Annie. Annie.

(In her patch of dark ANNIE, now in her nightgown, hurls a cup into a corner as though it were her grief, getting rid of its taste through her teeth.)

ANNIE: No! No pity, I won't have it.

(She comes to HELEN, prone on the floor.)

On either of us.

(She goes to her knees, but when she touches HELEN'S hand the child starts up awake, recoils, and scrambles away from her under the bed. ANNIE stares after her. She strikes her palm on the floor, with passion.)

I *will* touch you!

(She gets to her feet, and paces in a kind of anger around the bed, her hand in her hair, and confronting HELEN at each turn.)

How, how? How do I—

(ANNIE *stops. Then she calls out urgently, loudly.*)

Percy! Percy!

(*She moves swiftly to the drapes, at left.*)

Percy, wake up!

(PERCY'S *voice comes in a thick sleepy mumble, unintelligible.*)

Get out of bed and come in here, I need you.

(ANNIE *darts away, finds and strikes a match, and touches it to the hanging lamp; the lights come up dimly in the room, and* PERCY *stands bare to the waist in torn overalls between the drapes, with eyes closed, swaying.* ANNIE *goes to him, pats his cheeks vigorously.*)

Percy. You awake?

PERCY: No'm.

ANNIE: How would you like to play a nice game?

PERCY: Whah?

ANNIE: With Helen. She's under the bed. Touch her hand.

(*She kneels* PERCY *down at the bed, thrusting his hand under it to contact* HELEN'S; HELEN *emits an animal sound and crawls to the opposite side, but commences sniffing.* ANNIE *rounds the bed with* PERCY *and thrusts his hand again at* HELEN; *this time* HELEN *clutches it, sniffs in recognition, and comes scrambling out after* PERCY, *to hug him with delight.* PERCY *alarmed struggles, and* HELEN'S *fingers go to his mouth.*)

PERCY: Lemme go. Lemme go—

(HELEN *fingers her own lips, as before, moving them in dumb imitation.*)

She tryin' talk. She gonna hit me—

ANNIE [GRIMLY]: She *can* talk. If she only knew, I'll show you how. She makes letters.

(She opens PERCY'S *other hand, and spells into it:)*

This one is C. C.

(She hits his palm with it a couple of times, her eyes upon HELEN *across him;* HELEN *gropes to feel what* PERCY'S *hand is doing, and when she encounters* ANNIE'S *she falls back from them.)*

She's mad at me now, though, she won't play. But she knows lots of letters. Here's another, A. C, a. C, a.

(But she is watching HELEN, *who comes groping, consumed with curiosity;* ANNIE *makes the letters in* PERCY'S *hand, and* HELEN *pokes to question what they are up to. Then* HELEN *snatches* PERCY'S *other hand, and quickly spells four letters into it.* ANNIE *follows them aloud.)*

C, a, k, e! She spells cake, she gets cake.

(She is swiftly over to the tray of food, to fetch cake and a jug of milk.)

She doesn't know yet it means this. Isn't it funny she knows how to spell it and doesn't *know* she knows?

(She breaks the cake in two pieces, and extends one to each; HELEN *rolls away from her offer.)*

Well, if she won't play it with me, I'll play it with you. Would you like to learn one she doesn't know?

PERCY: No'm.

(But ANNIE *seizes his wrist, and spells to him.)*

ANNIE: M, i, l, k. M is this. I, that's an easy one, just the little finger. L is this—

(And HELEN *comes back with her hand, to feel the new word.* ANNIE *brushes her away, and continues spelling aloud to* PERCY. HELEN'S *hand comes back again, and tries to get in;* ANNIE *brushes it away again.* HELEN'S *hand insists, and* ANNIE *puts it away rudely.)*

No, why should I talk to you? I'm teaching Percy a new word. L. K is this—

*(*HELEN *now yanks their hands apart; she butts* PERCY *away, and thrusts her palm out insistently.* ANNIE'S *eyes are bright, with glee.)*

Ho, you're *jealous,* are you!

*(*HELEN'S *hand waits, intractably waits.)*

All *right.*

*(*ANNIE *spells into it,* milk; *and* HELEN *after a moment spells it back to* ANNIE. ANNIE *takes her hand, with her whole face shining. She gives a great sigh.)*

Good! So I'm finally back to where I can touch you, hm? Touch and go! No love lost, but here we go.

(She puts the jug of milk into HELEN'S *hand and squeezes* PERCY'S *shoulder.)*

You can go to bed now, you've earned your sleep. Thank you.

*(*PERCY *stumbling up weaves his way out through the drapes.* HELEN *finishes drinking, and holds the jug out, for* ANNIE; *when* ANNIE *takes it,* HELEN *crawls onto the bed, and makes for sleep.* ANNIE *stands, looks down at her.)*

Now all I have to teach you is—one word. Everything.

(She sets the jug down. On the floor now ANNIE *spies the doll, stoops to pick it up, and with it dangling in her hand, turns off the lamp. A shaft of moonlight is left on* HELEN *in the bed, and*

a second shaft on the rocking chair; and ANNIE, *after putting off her smoked glasses, sits in the rocker with the doll. She is rather happy, and dangles the doll on her knee, and it makes its momma sound.* ANNIE *whispers to it in mock solicitude.)*

Hush, little baby. Don't—say a word—

(She lays it against her shoulder, and begins rocking with it, patting its diminutive behind; she talks the lullaby to it, humorously at first.)

> Momma's gonna buy you—a mockingbird:
> If that—mockingbird don't sing—

(The rhythm of the rocking takes her into the tune, softly, and more tenderly.)

> Momma's gonna buy you a diamond ring:
> If that diamond ring turns to brass—

(A third shaft of moonlight outside now rises to pick out JAMES *at the main house, with one foot on the porch step; he turns his body, as if hearing the song.)*

> Momma's gonna buy you a looking-glass:
> If that looking-glass gets broke—

(In the family room a fourth shaft picks out KELLER *seated at the table, in thought; and he, too, lifts his head, as if hearing.)*

> Momma's gonna buy you a billy goat:
> If that billy goat won't pull—

(The fifth shaft is upstairs in ANNIE'S *room, and picks out* KATE, *pacing there; and she halts, turning her head, too, as if hearing.)*

> Momma's gonna buy you a cart and bull:
> If that cart and bull turns over,
> Momma's gonna buy you a dog named Rover;
> If that dog named Rover won't bark—

(With the shafts of moonlight on HELEN, *and* JAMES, *and* KELLER, *and* KATE, *all moveless, and* ANNIE *rocking the doll, the curtain ends the act.)*

ANNE BANCROFT **and** PATTY DUKE

ANNIE: All right, Miss O'Sullivan. Let's begin with doll.

PATTY DUKE and ANNE BANCROFT

ANNIE: She ate from her own plate.... She ate with a spoon. Herself.... And she folded her napkin.... The room's a wreck, but her napkin is folded.

ANNE BANCROFT and PATTY DUKE

ANNIE: Water. W, a, t, e, r. Water. It has a — name — (And now the miracle happens. HELEN drops the pitcher on the slab under the spout, it shatters. She stands transfixed. ANNIE freezes on the pump handle; there is a change in the sundown light, and with it a change in HELEN'S face... and her lips tremble, trying to remember something the muscles around them once knew, till at last it finds its way out, painfully, a baby sound buried under the debris of years of dumbness.)
HELEN: Wah. Wah.

ANNE BANCROFT, PATTY DUKE, TORIN THATCHER and PATRICIA NEAL

ANNIE: Mother.... Papa. —She <u>knows</u>!... Teacher.... I, love, Helen. Forever, and— ... —ever.

Photo credits: Fred Fehl

ACT THREE

ACT III

The stage is totally dark, until we see ANNIE *and* HELEN *silhouetted on the bed in the garden house.* ANNIE'S *voice is audible, very patient, and worn; it has been saying this for a long time.*

ANNIE: Water, Helen. This is water. W, a, t, e, r. It has a *name*.

(A silence. Then:)

Egg, e, g, g. It has a *name*, the name stands for the thing. Oh, it's so simple, simple as birth, to explain.

(The lights have commenced to rise, not on the garden house but on the homestead. Then:)

Helen, Helen, the chick *has* to come out of its shell, sometime. You come out, too.

(In the bedroom upstairs, we see VINEY *unhurriedly washing the window, dusting, turning the mattress, readying the room for use again; then in the family room a diminished group at one end of the table—*KATE, KELLER, JAMES*—finishing up a quiet breakfast; then outside, down right, the other Negro servant on his knees, assisted by* MARTHA, *working with a trowel around a new trellis and wheelbarrow. The scene is one of everyday calm, and all are oblivious to* ANNIE'S *voice.)*

There's only one way out, for you, and it's language. To learn that your fingers can talk. And say anything, anything you can name. This is mug. Mug, m, u, g. Helen, it has a *name*. It—has—a —*name*—

*(*KATE *rises from the table.)*

KELLER [GENTLY]: You haven't eaten, Katie.

KATE [SMILES, SHAKES HER HEAD]: I haven't the appetite. I'm too —restless, I can't sit to it.

KELLER: You should eat, my dear. It will be a long day, waiting.

JAMES [LIGHTLY]: But it's been a short two weeks. I never thought life could be so—noiseless, went much too quickly for me.

(KATE *and* KELLER *gaze at him, in silence.* JAMES *becomes uncomfortable.*)

ANNIE: C, a, r, d. Card. C, a—

JAMES: Well, the house has been practically normal, hasn't it?

KELLER [HARSHLY]: Jimmie.

JAMES: Is it wrong to enjoy a quiet breakfast, after five years? And you two even seem to enjoy each other—

KELLER: It could be even more noiseless, Jimmie, without your tongue running every minute. Haven't you enough feeling to imagine what Katie has been undergoing, ever since—

(KATE *stops him, with her hand on his arm.*)

KATE: Captain.

(*To* JAMES.)

It's true. The two weeks have been normal, quiet, all you say. But not short. Interminable.

(*She rises, and wanders out; she pauses on the porch steps, gazing toward the garden house.*)

ANNIE [FADING]: W, a, t, e, r. But it means *this.* W, a, t, e, r. *This.* W, a, t—

JAMES: I only meant that Miss Sullivan is a boon. Of contention, though, it seems.

KELLER [HEAVILY]: If and when you're a parent, Jimmie, you will understand what separation means. A mother loses a—protector.

JAMES [BAFFLED]: Hm?

KELLER: You'll learn, we don't just keep our children safe. They keep us safe.

(He rises, with his empty coffee cup and saucer.)

There are of course all kinds of separation, Katie has lived with one kind for five years. And another is disappointment. In a child.

(He goes with the cup out the rear door. JAMES sits for a long moment of stillness. In the garden house the lights commence to come up; ANNIE, haggard at the table, is writing a letter, her face again almost in contact with the stationery; HELEN, apart on the stool, and for the first time as clean and neat as a button, is quietly crocheting an endless chain of wool, which snakes all around the room.)

ANNIE: "I, feel, every, day, more, and, more, in—"

(She pauses, and turns the pages of a dictionary open before her; her finger descends the words to a full stop. She elevates her eyebrows, then copies the word.)

"—adequate."

(In the main house JAMES pushes up, and goes to the front doorway, after KATE.)

JAMES: Kate?

(KATE turns her glance. JAMES is rather weary.)

I'm sorry. Open my mouth, like that fairy tale, frogs jump out.

KATE: No. It has been better. For everyone.

(She starts away, up center.)

ANNIE [WRITING]: "If, only, there, were, someone, to, help, me, I, need, a, teacher, as, much, as, Helen—"

JAMES: Kate.

(KATE *halts, waits.*)

What does he want from me?

KATE: That's not the question. Stand up to the world, Jimmie, that comes first.

JAMES [A PAUSE, WRYLY]: But the world is him.

KATE: Yes. And no one can do it for you.

JAMES: Kate.

(*His voice is humble.*)

At least we— Could you—be my friend?

KATE: I am.

(KATE *turns to wander, up back of the garden house.* ANNIE'S *murmur comes at once; the lights begin to die on the main house.*)

ANNIE: "—my, mind, is, undisiplined, full, of, skips, and, jumps, and—"

(*She halts, rereads, frowns.*)

Hm.

(ANNIE *puts her nose again in the dictionary, flips back to an earlier page, and fingers down the words;* KATE *presently comes down toward the bay window with a trayful of food.*)

Disinter—disinterested—disjoin—dis—

(*She backtracks, indignant.*)

Disinterested, disjoin— Where's disipline?

(She goes a page or two back, searching with her finger, muttering.)

What a dictionary, have to know how to spell it before you can look up how to spell it, disciple, *discipline!* Diskipline.

(She corrects the word in her letter.)

Undisciplined.

(But her eyes are bothering her, she closes them in exhaustion and gently fingers the eyelids. KATE *watches her through the window.)*

KATE: What are you doing to your eyes?

*(*ANNIE *glances around; she puts her smoked glasses on, and gets up to come over, assuming a cheerful energy.)*

ANNIE: It's worse on my vanity! I'm learning to spell. It's like a surprise party, the most unexpected characters turn up.

KATE: You're not to overwork your eyes, Miss Annie.

ANNIE: Well.

(She takes the tray, sets it on her chair, and carries chair and tray to HELEN.*)*

Whatever I spell to Helen I'd better spell right.

KATE [ALMOST WISTFUL]: How—serene she is.

ANNIE: She learned this stitch yesterday. Now I can't get her to stop!

(She disentangles one foot from the wool chain, and sets the chair before HELEN. HELEN *at its contact with her knee feels the plate, promptly sets her crocheting down, and tucks the napkin in at her neck, but* ANNIE *withholds the spoon; when* HELEN *finds it missing, she folds her hands in her lap, and quietly waits.* ANNIE *twinkles at* KATE *with mock devoutness.)*

Such a little lady, she'd sooner starve than eat with her fingers.

(She gives HELEN *the spoon, and* HELEN *begins to eat, neatly.)*

KATE: You've taught her so much, these two weeks. I would never have—

ANNIE: Not enough.

(She is suddenly gloomy, shakes her head.)

Obedience isn't enough. Well, she learned two nouns this morning, key and water, brings her up to eighteen nouns and three verbs.

KATE [HESITANT]: But—not—

ANNIE: No. Not that they mean things. It's still a finger-game, no meaning.

(She turns to KATE, *abruptly.)*

Mrs. Keller—

(But she defers it; she comes back, to sit in the bay and lift her hand.)

Shall we play our finger-game?

KATE: How will she learn it?

ANNIE: It will come.

(She spells a word; KATE *does not respond.)*

KATE: How?

ANNIE [A PAUSE]: How does a bird learn to fly?

(She spells again.)

We're born to use words, like wings, it has to come.

KATE: How?

ANNIE [ANOTHER PAUSE, WEARILY]: All right. I don't know how.

(She pushes up her glasses, to rub her eyes.)

I've done everything I could think of. Whatever she's learned here—keeping herself clean, knitting, stringing beads, meals, setting-up exercises each morning, we climb trees, hunt eggs, yesterday a chick was born in her hands—all of it I spell, everything we do, we never stop spelling. I go to bed with—writer's cramp from talking so much!

KATE: I worry about you, Miss Annie. You must rest.

ANNIE: Now? She spells back in her *sleep*, her fingers make letters when she doesn't know! In her bones those five fingers know, that hand aches to—speak out, and something in her mind is asleep, how do I—nudge that awake? That's the one question.

KATE: With no answer.

ANNIE [LONG PAUSE]: Except keep at it. Like this.

(She again begins spelling—I, need—and KATE'S *brows gather, following the words.)*

KATE: More—time?

(She glances at ANNIE, *who looks her in the eyes, silent.)*

Here?

ANNIE: Spell it.

(KATE *spells a word—no—shaking her head;* ANNIE *spells two words—why, not—back, with an impatient question in her eyes; and* KATE *moves her head in pain to answer it.)*

KATE: Because I can't—

ANNIE: Spell it! If she ever learns, you'll have a lot to tell each other, start now.

(KATE *painstakingly spells in air. In the midst of this the rear door opens, and* KELLER *enters with the setter* BELLE *in tow.)*

KELLER: Miss Sullivan? On my way to the office, I brought Helen a playmate—

ANNIE: Outside please, Captain Keller.

KELLER: My dear child, the two weeks are up today, surely you don't object to—

ANNIE [RISING]: They're not up till six o'clock.

KELLER [INDULGENT]: Oh, now. What difference can a fraction of one day—

ANNIE: An agreement is an agreement. Now you've been very good, I'm sure you can keep it up for a few more hours.

(*She escorts* KELLER *by the arm over the threshold; he obeys, leaving* BELLE.)

KELLER: Miss Sullivan, you are a tyrant.

ANNIE: Likewise, I'm sure. You can stand there, and close the door if she comes.

KATE: I don't think you know how eager we are to have her back in our arms—

ANNIE: I do know, it's my main worry.

KELLER: It's like expecting a new child in the house. Well, she *is*, so—composed, so—

(*Gently*)

Attractive. You've done wonders for her, Miss Sullivan.

ANNIE [NOT A QUESTION]: Have I.

KELLER: If there's anything you want from us in repayment tell us, it will be a privilege to—

ANNIE: I just told Mrs. Keller. I want more time.

KATE: Miss Annie—

ANNIE: Another week.

(HELEN *lifts her head, and begins to sniff.*)

KELLER: We miss the child. *I* miss her, I'm glad to say, that's a different debt I owe you—

ANNIE: Pay it to Helen. Give *her* another week.

KATE [GENTLY]: Doesn't she miss us?

KELLER: Of course she does. What a wrench this unexplainable— exile must be to her, can you say it's not?

ANNIE: No. But I—

(HELEN *is off the stool, to grope about the room; when she encounters* BELLE, *she throws her arms around the dog's neck in delight.*)

KATE: Doesn't she need affection too, Miss Annie?

ANNIE [WAVERING]: She—never shows me she needs it, she won't have any—caressing or—

KATE: But you're not her mother.

KELLER: And what would another week accomplish? We are more than satisfied, you've done more than we ever thought possible, taught her constructive—

ANNIE: I can't promise anything. All I can—

KELLER [NO BREAK]: —things to do, to behave like—even look like—a human child, so manageable, contented, cleaner, more—

ANNIE [WITHERING]: Cleaner.

KELLER: Well. We say cleanliness is next to godliness, Miss—

ANNIE: Cleanliness is next to nothing, she has to learn that everything has its name! That words can be her *eyes,* to everything in the world outside her, and inside too, what is she without words? With them she can think, have ideas, be reached, there's not a thought or fact in the world that can't be hers. You publish a newspaper, Captain Keller, do I have to tell you what words are? And she has them already—

KELLER: Miss Sullivan.

ANNIE: —eighteen nouns and three verbs, they're in her fingers now, I need only time to push *one* of them into her mind! One, and everything under the sun will follow. Don't you see what she's learned here is only clearing the way for that? I can't risk her unlearning it, give me more time alone with her, another week to—

KELLER: Look.

(He points, and ANNIE *turns.* HELEN *is playing with* BELLE'S *claws; she makes letters with her fingers, shows them to* BELLE, *waits with her palm, then manipulates the dog's claws.)*

What is she spelling?

(A silence.)

KATE: Water?

*(*ANNIE *nods.)*

KELLER: Teaching a dog to spell.

(A pause.)

The dog doesn't know what she means, any more than she knows what you mean, Miss Sullivan. I think you ask too much, of her and yourself. God may not have meant Helen to have the —eyes you speak of.

ANNIE [TONELESS]: I mean her to.

KELLER [CURIOUSLY]: What is it to you?

*(*ANNIE'S *head comes slowly up.)*

You make us see how we indulge her for our sake. Is the opposite true, for you?

ANNIE [THEN]: Half a week?

KELLER: An agreement *is* an agreement.

ANNIE: Mrs. Keller?

KATE [SIMPLY]: I want her back.

(A wait; ANNIE then lets her hands drop in surrender, and nods.)

KELLER: I'll send Viney over to help you pack.

ANNIE: Not until six o'clock. I have her till six o'clock.

KELLER [CONSENTING]: Six o'clock. Come, Katie.

(KATE leaving the window joins him around back, while KELLER closes the door; they are shut out.

Only the garden house is daylit now, and the light on it is narrowing down. ANNIE stands watching HELEN work BELLE'S claws. Then she settles beside them on her knees, and stops HELEN'S hand.)

ANNIE [GENTLY]: No.

(She shakes her head, with HELEN'S hand to her face, then spells.)

Dog. D, o, g. Dog.

(She touches HELEN'S hand to BELLE. HELEN dutifully pats the dog's head, and resumes spelling to its paw.)

Not water.

(ANNIE rolls to her feet, brings a tumbler of water back from the tray, and kneels with it, to seize HELEN'S hand and spell.)

HERE. WATER. *Water*

(She thrusts HELEN'S hand into the tumbler. HELEN lifts her hand out dripping, wipes it daintily on BELLE'S hide, and taking the tumbler from ANNIE, endeavors to thrust BELLE'S paw into it. ANNIE sits watching, wearily.)

I don't know how to tell you. Not a soul in the world knows how to tell you. Helen, Helen.

(She bends in compassion to touch her lips to HELEN'S *temple, and instantly* HELEN *pauses, her hands off the dog, her head slightly averted. The lights are still narrowing, and* BELLE *slinks off. After a moment* ANNIE *sits back.)*

Yes, what's it to me? They're satisfied. Give them back their child and dog, both housebroken, everyone's satisfied. But me, and you.

*(*HELEN'S *hand comes out into the light, groping.)*

Reach. *Reach!*

*(*ANNIE *extending her own hand grips* HELEN'S; *the two hands are clasped, tense in the light, the rest of the room changing in shadow.)*

I wanted to teach you—oh, everything the earth is full of, Helen, everything on it that's ours for a wink and it's gone, and what we are on it, the—light we bring to it and leave behind in—words, why, you can see five thousand years back in a light of words, everything we feel, think, know—and share, in words, so not a soul is in darkness, or done with, even in the grave. And I know, I *know*, one word and I can—put the world in your hand—and whatever it is to me, I won't take less! How, how, how do I tell you that *this*—

(She spells.)

—means a *word*, and the word means this *thing*, wool?

(She thrusts the wool at HELEN'S *hand;* HELEN *sits, puzzled.* ANNIE *puts the crocheting aside.)*

Or this—s, t, o, o, l—means this *thing*, stool?

(She claps HELEN'S *palm to the stool.* HELEN *waits, uncomprehending.* ANNIE *snatches up her napkin, spells:)*

Napkin!

(She forces it on HELEN'S *hand, waits, discards it, lifts a fold of the child's dress, spells:)*

Dress!

(She lets it drop, spells:)

F, a, c, e, face!

(She draws HELEN'S *hand to her cheek, and pressing it there, staring into the child's responseless eyes, hears the distant belfry begin to toll, slowly: one, two, three, four, five, six.*

On the third stroke the lights stealing in around the garden house show us figures waiting: VINEY, *the other servant,* MARTHA, PERCY *at the drapes, and* JAMES *on the dim porch.* ANNIE *and* HELEN *remain, frozen. The chimes die away. Silently* PERCY *moves the drape-rod back out of sight;* VINEY *steps into the room—not using the door—and unmakes the bed; the other servant brings the wheelbarrow over, leaves it handy, rolls the bed off;* VINEY *puts the bed linens on top of a waiting boxful of* HELEN'S *toys, and loads the box on the wheelbarrow;* MARTHA *and* PERCY *take out the chairs, with the trayful, then the table; and* JAMES, *coming down and into the room, lifts* ANNIE'S *suitcase from its corner.* VINEY *and the other servant load the remaining odds and ends on the wheelbarrow, and the servant wheels it off.* VINEY *and the children departing leave only* JAMES *in the room with* ANNIE *and* HELEN. JAMES *studies the two of them, without mockery, and then, quietly going to the door and opening it, bears the suitcase out, and housewards. He leaves the door open.*

KATE *steps into the doorway, and stands.* ANNIE *lifting her gaze from* HELEN *sees her; she takes* HELEN'S *hand from her cheek, and returns it to the child's own, stroking it there twice, in her mother-sign, before spelling slowly into it:)*

M, o, t, h, e, r. Mother.

(HELEN *with her hand free strokes her cheek, suddenly forlorn.*
ANNIE *takes her hand again.*)

M, o, t, h—

(*But* KATE *is trembling with such impatience that her voice
breaks from her, harsh.*)

KATE: Let her *come!*

(ANNIE *lifts* HELEN *to her feet, with a turn, and gives her a little
push. Now* HELEN *begins groping, sensing something, trembling herself; and* KATE *falling one step in onto her knees clasps
her, kissing her.* HELEN *clutches her, tight as she can.* KATE *is
inarticulate, choked, repeating* HELEN'S *name again and again.
She wheels with her in her arms, to stumble away out the doorway;* ANNIE *stands unmoving, while* KATE *in a blind walk carries* HELEN *like a baby behind the main house, out of view.*

ANNIE *is now alone on the stage. She turns, gazing around at the
stripped room, bidding it silently farewell, impassively, like a
defeated general on the deserted battlefield. All that remains is
a stand with a basin of water; and here* ANNIE *takes up an
eyecup, bathes each of her eyes, empties the eyecup, drops it in
her purse, and tiredly locates her smoked glasses on the floor.
The lights alter subtly; in the act of putting on her glasses* ANNIE
*hears something that stops her, with head lifted. We hear it too,
the voices out of the past, including her own now, in a whisper:*)

BOY'S VOICE: You said we'd be together, forever— You promised,
forever and—*Annie!*

ANAGNOS' VOICE: But that battle is dead and done with, why not
let it stay buried?

ANNIE'S VOICE [WHISPERING]: I think God must owe me a resurrection.

ANAGNOS' VOICE: What?

(*A pause, and* ANNIE *answers it herself, heavily.*)

ANNIE: And I owe God one.

BOY'S VOICE: Forever and ever—

(ANNIE *shakes her head.*)

—forever, and ever, and—

(ANNIE *covers her ears.*)

—forever, and ever, and ever—

(*It pursues* ANNIE; *she flees to snatch up her purse, wheels to the doorway, and* KELLER *is standing in it. The lights have lost their special color.*)

KELLER: Miss—Annie.

(*He has an envelope in his fingers.*)

I've been waiting to give you this.

ANNIE [AFTER A BREATH]: What?

KELLER: Your first month's salary.

(*He puts it in her hand.*)

With many more to come, I trust. It doesn't express what we feel, it doesn't pay our debt. For what you've done.

ANNIE: What have I done?

KELLER: Taken a wild thing, and given us back a child.

ANNIE [PRESENTLY]: I taught her one thing, no. Don't do this, don't do that—

KELLER: It's more than all of us could, in all the years we—

ANNIE: I wanted to teach her what language is. I wanted to teach her yes.

KELLER: You will have time.

ANNIE: I don't know how. I know without it to do nothing but obey is—no gift, obedience without understanding is a—blindness, too. Is that all I've wished on her?

KELLER [GENTLY]: No, no—

ANNIE: Maybe. I don't know what else to do. Simply go on, keep doing what I've done, and have—faith that inside she's— That inside it's waiting. Like water, underground. All I can do is keep on.

KELLER: It's enough. For us.

ANNIE: You can help, Captain Keller.

KELLER: How?

ANNIE: Even learning no has been at a cost. Of much trouble and pain. Don't undo it.

KELLER: Why should we wish to—

ANNIE [ABRUPTLY]: The world isn't an easy place for anyone, I don't want her just to obey but to let her have her way in everything is a lie, to *her*, I can't—

(Her eyes fill, it takes her by surprise, and she laughs through it.)

And I don't even love her, she's not my child! Well. You've got to stand between that lie and her.

KELLER: We'll try.

ANNIE: Because *I* will. As long as you let me stay, that's one promise I'll keep.

KELLER: Agreed. We've learned something too, I hope.

(A pause)

Won't you come now, to supper?

ANNIE: Yes.

(She wags the envelope, ruefully.)

Why doesn't God pay His debts each month?

KELLER: I beg your pardon?

ANNIE: Nothing. I used to wonder how I could—

(The lights are fading on them, simultaneously rising on the family room of the main house, where VINEY *is polishing glassware at the table set for dinner.)*

—earn a living.

KELLER: Oh, you do.

ANNIE: I really do. Now the question is, can I survive it!

*(*KELLER *smiles, offers his arm.)*

KELLER: May I?

*(*ANNIE *takes it, and the lights lose them as he escorts her out.*

Now in the family room the rear door opens, and HELEN *steps in. She stands a moment, then sniffs in one deep grateful breath, and her hands go out vigorously to familiar things, over the door panels, and to the chairs around the table, and over the silverware on the table, until she meets* VINEY; *she pats her flank approvingly.)*

VINEY: Oh, we glad to have you back too, prob'ly.

*(*HELEN *hurries groping to the front door, opens and closes it, removes its key, opens and closes it again to be sure it is unlocked, gropes back to the rear door and repeats the procedure, removing its key and hugging herself gleefully.*

AUNT EV *is next in by the rear door, with a relish tray; she bends to kiss* HELEN'S *cheek.* HELEN *finds* KATE *behind her, and thrusts the keys at her.)*

KATE: What? Oh.

(To EV*)*

Keys.

(She pockets them, lets HELEN *feel them.)*

Yes, *I'll* keep the keys. I think we've had enough of locked doors, too.

*(*JAMES, *having earlier put* ANNIE'S *suitcase inside her door upstairs and taken himself out of view around the corner, now reappears and comes down the stairs as* ANNIE *and* KELLER *mount the porch steps. Following them into the family room, he pats* ANNIE'S *hair in passing, rather to her surprise.)*

JAMES: Evening, general.

(He takes his own chair opposite.

VINEY *bears the empty water pitcher out to the porch. The remaining suggestion of garden house is gone now, and the water pump is unobstructed;* VINEY *pumps water into the pitcher.*

KATE *surveying the table breaks the silence.)*

KATE: Will you say grace, Jimmie?

(They bow their heads, except for HELEN, *who palms her empty plate and then reaches to be sure her mother is there.* JAMES *considers a moment, glances across at* ANNIE, *lowers his head again, And obliges.)*

JAMES [LIGHTLY]: And Jacob was left alone, and wrestled with an angel until the breaking of the day; and the hollow of Jacob's thigh was out of joint, as he wrestled with him; and the angel said, Let me go, for the day breaketh. And Jacob said, I will not let thee go, except thou bless me. Amen.

*(*ANNIE *has lifted her eyes suspiciously at* JAMES, *who winks expressionlessly and inclines his head to* HELEN.)*

Oh, you angel.

(The others lift their faces; VINEY *returns with the pitcher, setting it down near* KATE, *then goes out the rear door; and* ANNIE *puts a napkin around* HELEN.)

AUNT EV: That's a very strange grace, James.

KELLER: Will you start the muffins, Ev?

JAMES: It's from the Good Book, isn't it?

AUNT EV [PASSING A PLATE]: Well, of course it is. Didn't you know?

JAMES: Yes, I knew.

KELLER [SERVING]: Ham, Miss Annie?

ANNIE: Please.

AUNT EV: Then why ask?

JAMES: I meant it *is* from the Good Book, and therefore a fitting grace.

AUNT EV: Well. I don't know about *that.*

KATE [WITH THE PITCHER]: Miss Annie?

ANNIE: Thank you.

AUNT EV: There's an awful *lot* of things in the Good Book that I wouldn't care to hear just before eating.

(When ANNIE *reaches for the pitcher,* HELEN *removes her napkin and drops it to the floor.* ANNIE *is filling* HELEN'S *glass when she notices it; she considers* HELEN'S *bland expression a moment, then bends, retrieves it, and tucks it around* HELEN'S *neck again.)*

JAMES: Well, fitting in the sense that Jacob's thigh was out of joint, and so is this piggie's.

AUNT EV: I declare, James—

KATE: Pickles, Aunt Ev?

AUNT EV: Oh, I should say so, you know my opinion of your pickles—

KATE: This is the end of them, I'm afraid. I didn't put up nearly enough last summer, this year I intend to—

(She interrupts herself, seeing HELEN *deliberately lift off her napkin and drop it again to the floor. She bends to retrieve it, but* ANNIE *stops her arm.)*

KELLER [NOT NOTICING]: Reverend looked in at the office today to complain his hens have stopped laying. Poor fellow, *he* was out of joint, all he could—

(He stops too, to frown down the table at KATE, HELEN, *and* ANNIE *in turn, all suspended in mid-motion.)*

JAMES [NOT NOTICING]: I've always suspected those hens.

AUNT EV: Of what?

JAMES: I think they're Papist. Has he tried—

(He stops, too, following KELLER'S *eyes.* ANNIE *now stops to pick the napkin up.)*

AUNT EV: James, now you're pulling my—lower extremity, the first thing you know we'll be—

(She stops, too, hearing herself in the silence. ANNIE, *with everyone now watching, for the third time puts the napkin on* HELEN. HELEN *yanks it off, and throws it down.* ANNIE *rises, lifts* HELEN'S *plate, and bears it away.* HELEN, *feeling it gone, slides down and commences to kick up under the table; the dishes jump.* ANNIE *contemplates this for a moment, then coming back takes* HELEN'S *wrists firmly and swings her off the chair.* HELEN *struggling gets one hand free, and catches at her mother's skirt; when* KATE *takes her by the shoulders,* HELEN *hangs quiet.)*

KATE: Miss Annie.

ANNIE: No.

KATE [A PAUSE]: It's a very special day.

ANNIE [GRIMLY]: It will be, when I give in to that.

(She tries to disengage HELEN'S *hand;* KATE *lays hers on* AN-NIE'S.)*

KATE: Please. I've hardly had a chance to welcome her home—

ANNIE: Captain Keller.

KELLER [EMBARRASSED]: Oh. Katie, we—had a little talk, Miss Annie feels that if we indulge Helen in these—

AUNT EV: But what's the child done?

ANNIE: She's learned not to throw things on the floor and kick. It took us the best part of two weeks and—

AUNT EV: But only a napkin, it's not as if it were breakable!

ANNIE: And everything she's learned *is?* Mrs. Keller, I don't think we should—play tug-of-war for her, either give her to me or you keep her from kicking.

KATE: What do you wish to do?

ANNIE: Let me take her from the table.

AUNT EV: Oh, let her stay, my goodness, she's only a child, she doesn't have to wear a napkin if she doesn't want to her first evening—

ANNIE [LEVEL]: And ask outsiders not to interfere.

AUNT EV [ASTONISHED]: Out—outsi— I'm the child's *aunt!*

KATE [DISTRESSED]: Will once hurt so much, Miss Annie? I've—made all Helen's favorite foods, tonight.

(A pause)

KELLER [GENTLY]: It's a homecoming party, Miss Annie.

(ANNIE *after a moment releases* HELEN. *But she cannot accept it, at her own chair she shakes her head and turns back, intent on* KATE.)

ANNIE: She's testing you. You realize?

JAMES [TO ANNIE]: She's testing you.

KELLER: Jimmie, be quiet.

(JAMES *sits, tense.*)

Now she's home, naturally she—

ANNIE: And wants to see what will happen. At your hands. I said it was my main worry, is this what you promised me not half an hour ago?

KELLER [REASONABLY]: But she's *not* kicking, now—

ANNIE: And not learning not to. Mrs. Keller, teaching her is bound to be painful, to everyone. I know it hurts to watch, but she'll live up to just what you demand of her, and no more.

JAMES [PALELY]: She's testing *you*.

KELLER [TESTILY]: Jimmie.

JAMES: I have an opinion, I think I should—

KELLER: No one's interested in hearing your opinion.

ANNIE: *I'm* interested, of course she's testing me. Let me keep her to what she's learned and she'll go on learning from me. Take her out of my hands and it all comes apart.

(KATE *closes her eyes, digesting it;* ANNIE *sits again, with a brief comment for her.*)

Be bountiful, it's at her expense.

(*She turns to* JAMES, *flatly.*)

Please pass me more of—her favorite foods.

(*Then* KATE *lifts* HELEN'S *hand, and turning her toward* ANNIE, *surrenders her;* HELEN *makes for her own chair.*)

KATE [LOW]: Take her, Miss Annie.

ANNIE [THEN]: Thank you.

(*But the moment* ANNIE *rising reaches for her hand,* HELEN *begins to fight and kick, clutching to the tablecloth, and utter-*

ing laments. ANNIE *again tries to loosen her hand, and* KELLER *rises.)*

KELLER [TOLERANT]: I'm afraid you're the difficulty, Miss Annie. Now I'll keep her to what she's learned, you're quite right there—

(He takes HELEN'S *hands from* ANNIE, *pats them;* HELEN *quiets down.)*

—but I don't see that we need send her from the table, after all, she's the guest of honor. Bring her plate back.

ANNIE: If she was a seeing child, none of you would tolerate one—

KELLER: Well, she's not, I think some compromise is called for. Bring her plate, please.

*(*ANNIE'S *jaw sets, but she restores the plate, while* KELLER *fastens the napkin around* HELEN'S *neck; she permits it.)*

There. It's not unnatural, most of us take some aversion to our teachers, and occasionally another hand can smooth things out.

(He puts a fork in HELEN'S *hand;* HELEN *takes it. Genially:)*

Now. Shall we start all over?

(He goes back around the table, and sits. ANNIE *stands watching.* HELEN *is motionless, thinking things through, until with a wicked glee she deliberately flings the fork on the floor. After another moment she plunges her hand into her food, and crams a fistful into her mouth.)*

JAMES [WEARILY]: I think we've started all over—

*(*KELLER *shoots a glare at him, as* HELEN *plunges her other hand into* ANNIE'S *plate.* ANNIE *at once moves in, to grasp her wrist, and* HELEN *flinging out a hand encounters the pitcher; she swings with it at* ANNIE; ANNIE *falling back blocks it with an elbow, but the water flies over her dress.* ANNIE *gets her breath, then snatches the pitcher away in one hand, hoists* HELEN *up*

bodily under the other arm, and starts to carry her out, kicking.
KELLER *stands.)*

ANNIE [SAVAGELY POLITE]: Don't get up!

KELLER: Where are you going?

ANNIE: Don't smooth anything else out for me, don't interfere in
any way! I treat her like a seeing child because I *ask* her to see, I
expect her to see, don't undo what I do!

KELLER: Where are you taking her?

ANNIE: To make her fill this pitcher again!

(She thrusts out with HELEN *under her arm, but* HELEN *escapes
up the stairs and* ANNIE *runs after her.* KELLER *stands rigid.*
AUNT EV *is astounded.)*

AUNT EV: You let her speak to you like that, Arthur? A creature
who *works* for you?

KELLER [ANGRILY]: No. I don't.

(He is starting after ANNIE *when* JAMES, *on his feet with shaky
resolve, interposes his chair between them in* KELLER'S *path.)*

JAMES: Let her go.

KELLER: What!

JAMES [A SWALLOW]: I said—let her go. She's right.

*(*KELLER *glares at the chair and him.* JAMES *takes a deep breath,
then headlong:)*

She's right, Kate's right, I'm right, and you're wrong. If you
drive her away from here it will be over my dead—chair, has it
never occurred to you that on one occasion you might be con-
summately wrong?

*(*KELLER'S *stare is unbelieving, even a little fascinated.* KATE
rises in trepidation, to mediate.)

KATE: Captain.

(KELLER stops her with his raised hand; his eyes stay on JAMES'
pale face, for a long hold. When he finally finds his voice, it is
gruff.)

KELLER: Sit down, everyone.

(He sits. KATE sits. JAMES holds onto his chair. KELLER speaks
mildly.)

Please sit down, Jimmie.

(JAMES sits, and a moveless silence prevails; KELLER'S eyes do
not leave him.

ANNIE *has pulled* HELEN *downstairs again by one hand, the*
pitcher in her other hand, down the porch steps, and across the
yard to the pump. She puts HELEN'S *hand on the pump handle,*
grimly.)

ANNIE: All right. Pump.

(HELEN touches her cheek, waits uncertainly.)

No, she's not here. Pump!

(She forces HELEN'S *hand to work the handle, then lets go. And*
HELEN *obeys. She pumps till the water comes, then* ANNIE *puts*
the pitcher in her other hand and guides it under the spout, and
the water tumbling half into and half around the pitcher douses
HELEN'S *hand.* ANNIE *takes over the handle to keep water com-*
ing, and does automatically what she has done so many times
before, spells into HELEN'S *free palm:)*

Water. W, a, t, e, r. *Water.* It has a—*name*—

(And now the miracle happens. HELEN *drops the pitcher on the*
slab under the spout, it shatters. She stands transfixed. ANNIE
freezes on the pump handle: there is a change in the sundown
light, and with it a change in HELEN'S *face, some light coming*

*into it we have never seen there, some struggle in the depths
behind it; and her lips tremble, trying to remember something
the muscles around them once knew, till at last it finds its way
out, painfully, a baby sound buried under the debris of years of
dumbness.)*

HELEN: Wah. Wah.

(And again, with great effort)

Wah. Wah.

(HELEN *plunges her hand into the dwindling water, spells into
her own palm. Then she gropes frantically,* ANNIE *reaches for
her hand, and* HELEN *spells into* ANNIE'S *hand.)*

ANNIE [WHISPERING]: Yes.

(HELEN *spells into it again.)*

Yes!

(HELEN *grabs at the handle, pumps for more water, plunges her
hand into its spurt and grabs* ANNIE'S *to spell it again.)*

Yes! Oh, my dear—

(She falls to her knees to clasp HELEN'S *hand, but* HELEN *pulls it
free, stands almost bewildered, then drops to the ground, pats it
swiftly, holds up her palm, imperious.* ANNIE *spells into it:)*

Ground.

(HELEN *spells it back.)*

Yes!

(HELEN *whirls to the pump, pats it, holds up her palm, and*
ANNIE *spells into it.)*

Pump.

(HELEN *spells it back.*)

Yes! Yes!

(Now HELEN *is in such an excitement she is possessed, wild, trembling, cannot be still, turns, runs, falls on the porch steps, claps it, reaches out her palm, and* ANNIE *is at it instantly to spell:)*

Step.

(HELEN *has no time to spell back now, she whirls groping, to touch anything, encounters the trellis, shakes it, thrusts out her palm, and* ANNIE *while spelling to her cries wildly at the house.)*

Trellis. Mrs. Keller! *Mrs. Keller!*

(Inside, KATE *starts to her feet.* HELEN *scrambles back onto the porch, groping, and finds the bell string, tugs it; the bell rings, the distant chimes begin tolling the hour, all the bells in town seem to break into speech while* HELEN *reaches out and* ANNIE *spells feverishly into her hand.* KATE *hurries out, with* KELLER *after her;* AUNT EV *is on her feet, to peer out the window; only* JAMES *remains at the table, and with a napkin wipes his damp brow. From up right and left the servants—*VINEY, *the two Negro children, the other servant—run in, and stand watching from a distance as* HELEN, *ringing the bell, with her other hand encounters her mother's skirt; when she throws a hand out,* ANNIE *spells into it:)*

Mother.

(KELLER *now seizes* HELEN'S *hand, she touches him, gestures a hand, and* ANNIE *again spells:)*

Papa— She *knows!*

*(*KATE *and* KELLER *go to their knees, stammering, clutching* HELEN *to them, and* ANNIE *steps unsteadily back to watch the threesome,* HELEN *spelling wildly into* KATE'S *hand, then into*

KELLER'S, KATE *spelling back into* HELEN'S; *they cannot keep their hands off her, and rock her in their clasp.*

Then HELEN *gropes, feels nothing, turns all around, pulls free, and comes with both hands groping, to find* ANNIE. *She encounters* ANNIE'S *thighs,* ANNIE *kneels to her,* HELEN'S *hand pats* ANNIE'S *cheek impatiently, points a finger, and waits; and* ANNIE *spells into it:)*

Teacher.

(HELEN *spells it back, slowly;* ANNIE *nods.)*

Teacher.

(She holds HELEN'S *hand to her cheek. Presently* HELEN *withdraws it, not jerkily, only with reserve, and retreats a step. She stands thinking it over, then turns again and stumbles back to her parents. They try to embrace her, but she has something else in mind, it is to get the keys, and she hits* KATE'S *pocket until* KATE *digs them out for her.*

ANNIE *with her own load of emotion has retreated, her back turned, toward the pump, to sit;* KATE *moves to* HELEN, *touches her hand questioningly, and* HELEN *spells a word to her.* KATE *comprehends it, their first act of verbal communication, and she can hardly utter the word aloud, in wonder, gratitude, and deprivation; it is a moment in which she simultaneously finds and loses a child.)*

KATE: Teacher?

(ANNIE *turns; and* KATE, *facing* HELEN *in her direction by the shoulders, holds her back, holds her back, and then relinquishes her.* HELEN *feels her way across the yard, rather shyly, and when her moving hands touch* ANNIE'S *skirt she stops. Then she holds out the keys and places them in* ANNIE'S *hand. For a moment neither of them moves. Then* HELEN *slides into* ANNIE'S *arms, and lifting away her smoked glasses, kisses her on the cheek.* ANNIE *gathers her in.*

KATE *torn both ways turns from this, gestures the servants off, and makes her way into the house, on* KELLER'S *arm. The servants go, in separate directions.*

The lights are half down now, except over the pump. ANNIE *and* HELEN *are here, alone in the yard.* ANNIE *has found* HELEN'S *hand, almost without knowing it, and she spells slowly into it, her voice unsteady, whispering:)*

ANNIE: I, love, Helen.

(She clutches the child to her, tight this time, not spelling, whispering into her hair.)

Forever, and—

(She stops. The lights over the pump are taking on the color of the past, and it brings ANNIE'S *head up, her eyes opening, in fear; and as slowly as though drawn she rises, to listen, with her hand on* HELEN'S *shoulders. She waits, waits, listening with ears and eyes both, slowly here, slowly there: and hears only silence. There are no voices. The color passes on, and when her eyes come back to* HELEN *she can breathe the end of her phrase without fear:)*

—ever.

(In the family room KATE *has stood over the table, staring at* HELEN'S *plate, with* KELLER *at her shoulder; now* JAMES *takes a step to move her chair in, and* KATE *sits, with head erect, and* KELLER *inclines his head to* JAMES; *so it is* AUNT EV, *hesitant, and rather humble, who moves to the door.*

Outside HELEN *tugs at* ANNIE'S *hand, and* ANNIE *comes with it.* HELEN *pulls her toward the house; and hand in hand, they cross the yard, and ascend the porch steps, in the rising lights, to where* AUNT EV *is holding the door open for them.*

The curtain ends the play.)

MONDAY
AFTER THE
MIRACLE

MONDAY AFTER THE MIRACLE opened at the Eugene O'Neill Theatre in New York City on December 14, 1982, produced by Raymond Katz, Sandy Gallin and the John F. Kennedy Center. Direction was by Arthur Penn; sets by John Lee Beatty; lighting by F. Mitchell Dana; costumes by Carol Oditz; incidental music by Claude Kerry-White; production stage manager Susie Cordon.

The cast, in order of appearance, was as follows:

ANNIE	*Jane Alexander*
HELEN	*Karen Allen*
JOHN	*William Converse-Roberts*
PETE	*Matt McKenzie*
ED	*Joseph Warren*

Author's Note

The miracle in this title is of course identical with that in *The Miracle Worker*, a play I wrote a generation ago about a twenty-year-old named Annie Sullivan and a child she rescued from the "silent night" of the blind-deaf.

In the years that followed that astonishing double feat, of teaching and being taught, the pupil became world-famous as Helen Keller; most people had little idea of who the Miss Sullivan in the background was. Annie accepted this overshadowing with a sufficiency of grace, although once—when she was awarded an honorary degree and the reporters flocked around Helen—she said, "Even at my coronation Helen is queen."

This myopia in the public has continued into my day. *The Miracle Worker* is invariably identified as "the play about Helen Keller," and I have been asked a hundred times how I came to be so interested in her. I reply patiently I was never interested in her, the play is about her teacher, and for that reason is not named *The Miracle Workee*. Why I am so interested in her teacher is another question.

I have already told, how moving it was to encounter the young Annie in her letters. During her first years with Helen she wrote voluminously to a kind of foster-mother a step-by-step account—blow-by-blow would be more apt for the first month—of her tactics as a teacher; these were of her own devising, and extraordinary in invention, empathy, and doggedness. I fell in love with those letters. Who was this girl?—herself half-blinded in childhood by a disease of the unwashed poor, trachoma; left to the mercies of an alcoholic father when her mother died at twenty-eight; abandoned by him to a Massachusetts almshouse while he drifted west to get rich, and hanged himself in a Chicago flophouse; at fourteen a spitfire, talked herself into a Boston school for the blind where she could not write her name. Six years and nine eye operations later she graduated, took her first job as governess of the Keller child in Alabama, and in her palm wrote one of the great American stories.

It was no chore to be interested in her, or—prodded by my friend and director, Arthur Penn—to serve as scribe of that story. It exhilarated audiences in theatres around the world as it had me; a lost child had been wrestled with and brought into the human family, a cheering tale, and self-sufficient in its own terms. No one suspected it was also a parable about the teacher as something else.

Twenty years later I took another look at her life, wrote *Monday After the Miracle*—again pestered by Penn—and here I have come up with a new "play about Helen Keller." It still isn't.

My wife Margaret in her recent biography, *Clifford Odets: American Playwright,* has suggested that regardless of its subject every play includes in some way a concern for the playwright's own creativity. I think this is true, and on that level *The Miracle Worker* is a parable of the artist's struggle with his or her raw material; they rescue each other. This is the recurrent joy of art. The artist lives for these obsessive discoveries and conquests of portions of himself, which we as spectators participate in vicariously, and pay him for. But in the intervals he lives another life also, in the everyday, and how often the two are at war is seen in anyone with a mission; even Jesus slighted his mother. *Monday After the Miracle* is about that war.

Given a childless woman in her late thirties, with the fruits of success in one hand and the other empty, what then? Some fifteen years after the events they recounted, Annie's letters were edited for publication by a young critic named John Macy—I read him in my teens—whom she married, and invited into a household of three. Little is on record of that marriage; such documents as love-letters were destroyed, some by Annie, some by fire, and what went on in it is anybody's guess; *Monday After* is mine. All its major happenings are factual enough, although I have telescoped the years, and the characterizations are of course an act of the imagination.

I have resisted its being called a sequel, because anyone looking for more of the same will be much disappointed; it is a different work, a different mood, a different statement.

The Miracle Worker, which made people cry, was a comedy; and the grace of comedy is a white lie—that the story ends, and happily—which we take home to nourish our everyday lives wherein no story ends, short of death. It is no secret that man proposes, God disposes, and all of us who survive our youth live in a clutter of dreams gone wrong; we pick up the pieces and continue. So Annie. In *Monday After* the characters are older by twenty years, as is their playwright, and this is no comedy of youth's triumph; the eyeball ages, and vision darkens. Affirmations are still to be won, but the price is now known.

The play seems to ask, Is it worth it?—but there is no choice. And so there is no question; Mondays are as real as ecstasies, but no realer, we live both. And if this play is darker bread than its predecessor it is not I hope, without its own nourishment.

W. G.

ANNIE
HELEN
JOHN
PETE
ED

The play takes place in the early part of this century in the Boston area—a Cambridge cottage, then a house in Wrentham.

ACT ONE

ACT I

Two upper platforms with beds; steps between descending to stage proper and minimal furniture—a small desk with Braille writer, a couch, chairs. Beyond, an outside area with clothesline. Trees visible at rear.

MUSIC.

AT THE CLOTHESLINE, ANNIE—HER SLEEVES ROLLED UP, HER HAIR UNKEMPT, AN ATTRACTIVE SLATTERN IN HER LATE THIRTIES —IS UNPINNING CLOTHES OVER A WASHBASKET.

HELEN, IN HER EARLY TWENTIES, IS SEATED WORKING AT THE BRAILLE WRITER.

DOWNSTAGE OF HER, A YOUNG MAN—JOHN, TWENTY-FIVE, TWEEDY, BOOKS IN POCKET, AND A SPRIG OF LILAC IN HAND— ENTERS TO TUG AT A DOORBELL (NO DOOR).

INSIDE, HELEN TYPES. JOHN TUGS AGAIN, WAITS, AND IS TURNING TO LEAVE WHEN HE HEARS THE TYPING. MOVES A BIT CENTER, SQUATS AS THOUGH AT AN OPEN WINDOW.

JOHN: Hello.

(HELEN *types another word, oblivious, and rolls the page out;* JOHN *pokes his head in.*)

I said hello, I'm—

(HELEN *sits proofreading the page with her fingertips; and he straightens slowly. Then hears a pulley squeaking;* ANNIE *at the clothesline.*)

(JOHN *walks around to her. Thumbing back:*)

That's Helen Keller!

ANNIE: Yes?

JOHN: She's lovely.

ANNIE: Nothing today.

JOHN: What?

ANNIE: Nothing today, thank you.

JOHN [AMUSED]: Oh.

(He eyes her, working at the line.)

Well, you're not bad yourself, Maisie, why didn't you answer the door?

ANNIE: My name is not Maisie.

JOHN: A generic appellative, sweet.

(ANNIE *turns to stare.*)

Is Anne Mansfield Sullivan about? Miss Keller's pedagogue.

ANNIE: Yes; who are you?

JOHN: A friend to all downtrodden domestic help.

ANNIE [AMUSED]: Like me?

JOHN [DIGS IN HIS POCKET]: Have you read Karl Marx?

ANNIE: Who?

JOHN: Just discovered him. What *is* your name?

ANNIE: Bridget, of course.

JOHN: John Macy; I'm expected. Let's see—

ANNIE [KNOWS]: Oh.

JOHN: Wage-Labor And—Start with this, Bridget. Aren't you underpaid?

ANNIE: Indeed I am.

JOHN: And overworked.

ANNIE: I work like a slave.

JOHN: You don't have to live so. Old Karl analyzes all the reasons and gives the answer.

ANNIE [LOOKS INTO IT]: What's the answer?

JOHN: Revolution—

ANNIE: Revolution—

JOHN: —a beautiful word—

ANNIE: —don't tell me you're one of those?

JOHN: One of what?

ANNIE: Lunatics.

JOHN: The one thing that annoys me in the working class is how stupid it is. Made so, I know, by bad education—

ANNIE: Oh?

JOHN: —but you don't have to be exploited in this house; you say you are, why be so thick headed about your own interests? Read it, for God's sake.

ANNIE: It has no pictures.

(She gives it back—)

JOHN: Hopeless.

(—and precedes him into the kitchen area—)

Smells good.

ANNIE: I'm the cook too.

(—and to HELEN *typing; she touches her shoulder and spells by the manual alphabet—we hear these spelled words by the actors speaking over it, indicated as V.O.)*

This is John Macy, baby, who offered to help with the articles.
Take her hand, Mr. Macy, don't make a speech.

(JOHN *comes to take it, staring at* ANNIE; HELEN *explores his
hand.*)

JOHN: You are Annie Mansfield Sullivan.

HELEN [HER VOICE THICK, UNINFLECTED]: It's a, gracious offer.

ANNIE: You're not quite what we had in mind, Mr.—

JOHN [STARING]: What did she say?

ANNIE: It's a gracious offer.

JOHN: Oh. Forgive me, I'm a bit—embarrassed. And in awe
here—

ANNIE [V.O.]: I'm not sure he's suitable, baby.

HELEN [HAND OUT]: Let me, see him.

JOHN: What?

ANNIE: Bend, Mr. Macy.

(JOHN *bends;* HELEN *explores his face.*)

We read palms, faces—

HELEN: He is, talented.

JOHN: Thank you.

HELEN: And, knows it.

JOHN [AMUSED]: Well.

(*He straightens.*)

I *am* a good editorial hand. And Lenore said you need help.

ANNIE: I don't think we need an anarchist stuffing her head with
nonsense.

JOHN: Hey—

HELEN: Let us, talk.

JOHN: You led me on there, why?

ANNIE: Karl Marx isn't an everyday calling card.

JOHN: Look. There's a metropolis out there called the Athens of America. Complete with slavery.

ANNIE: Oh, come—

JOHN: I mean, a society which can't end hunger and illiteracy is nipping humanity in the bud. I believe in its flowering; so do you, or what's your life with this phenomenon? Loosen up!—I came to donate my services to Helen Keller, whom I admire, and they're purely technical. Can she use them or not?

ANNIE [A PAUSE]: Sit, Mr. Macy.

(She brings HELEN *to him on the couch, giving her the Braille pages.)*

JOHN: I did make a speech.

ANNIE: Out of hunger, no doubt. Did you eat?

JOHN: Yes.

ANNIE: This is next month's installment, to help with.

JOHN: It's, ah—bumpy going—

ANNIE: She types in Braille, of course.

HELEN: To, work! Do you read, Braille?

JOHN: No.

(Realizes; lifts HELEN'S *hand, shakes his head.)*

HELEN: I can't read back, what I type con, ventionally. You can't read, Braille. I perceive a, chasm.

JOHN: I'll learn.

(At a loss, he looks to ANNIE.)

HELEN: Will you, learn?

(JOHN *kisses her palm, nodding.*)

I see. Love, conquers all.

ANNIE: She lip-reads.

JOHN: Oh.

(He brings HELEN'S *fingers to his lips.)*

Am I legible?

HELEN: Oh, an open, book.

JOHN [TO ANNIE]: That's an odd sound.

ANNIE: She doesn't hear it.

JOHN: How did she learn to speak?

ANNIE: By imitating my tongue and throat muscles.

JOHN [PAUSE]: Wow. Not what anyone at Radcliffe would term your average student.

ANNIE: Above average, or she couldn't compete here; college itself is unprecedented, and we're aiming at honors. You have no beard.

JOHN: To learn Braille?

ANNIE: I thought your average professor had a beard.

JOHN: How does she manage the classwork?

ANNIE: I sit with her and spell.

JOHN: Ah.

(They sit together, ANNIE *spelling* JOHN'S *talk and her own to* HELEN.)

I'm not a professor.

ANNIE: Lenore said—

JOHN: I was an instructor. In English; Harvard.

ANNIE: She said Harvard.

JOHN: I left, I'm an editor at *Youth's Companion.*

ANNIE: Oh. That's even better.

JOHN: I'm not an editor, either.

HELEN: He grows vaguer and vaguer—

JOHN: I'm a writer. I have twenty books in my head; what I want to do first is a critical ground-clearing, get all the humbug out of American letters. As you did, with pedagogy. And start fresh, work out of authentic experience—

ANNIE: What stops you?

JOHN: Making a living. I mean, we've played the sedulous ape to Europe long enough; our literature has to get to our own life in the raw. What does this Boston crowd know of it?—Howells can't sit down with the American workingman, he doesn't speak his language.

ANNIE [DEMURE]: That is *your* specialty?

JOHN [SMILES]: I'm afraid you're—something of a witch.

ANNIE: Oh?

JOHN: Bewitching. Well, there's a whole new stream coming in; do you know *Maggie, A Girl of the Streets?*

HELEN: Do we?

ANNIE: I think she's a book.

JOHN: Stephen Crane, I'll bring it. There's a new man Dreiser worth watching, also interested in fallen women. It's the buried life in this country, the unprivileged, struggling for speech.

ANNIE [STOPS SPELLING]: Is that what Helen means to you?

JOHN: Well, now that I think of it, yes.

ANNIE: You *can* help us.

JOHN: Good.

ANNIE: But she's a risen woman.

JOHN: Thanks to you. But aren't you in a kind of bondage?

ANNIE: Bondage?

JOHN: To her?

(ANNIE *stares at him.*)

Let's discuss you.

(HELEN *waggles her hand;* ANNIE *spells briskly.*)

ANNIE: This magazine contract was a mistake; we needed the money, but we can't keep up with the college work and these articles both.

HELEN: The editor, is on our, neck.

JOHN: I've come to deliver you.

ANNIE: Not add to what Helen writes; it's her work.

HELEN: Prune. I get, lofty.

JOHN: I understand.

ANNIE: And help organize it; the Braille pages must be retyped, and proofread with her against the original—

HELEN [WAGGLING]: By this, alphabet.

ANNIE: —and collated. Yes, I'll teach you this language, it's a bit different from the workingman's.

(*She rises, amused.*)

In which ye're maybe not such an expert at all at all—

JOHN [RISES]: Meaning Irish.

ANNIE: Low life. In the raw. We rose together, a—mutual levitation—

HELEN: Au, revoir.

(ANNIE *walks* JOHN *to the doorbell area.*)

JOHN: She *is* a kind of genius.

ANNIE [DOESN'T LIKE THE WORD]: So people say. Sunday noon?

(JOHN *nods, offers his hand; they shake.*)

JOHN: Good night, Miss Sullivan.

ANNIE: I did mislead you; let's both overlook it.

JOHN: Certainly. Karl Marx was a copious writer; I'll bring something new of his each time.

ANNIE: That will be more punishment than I deserve.

JOHN: You have nothing to lose but your chains.

(*He gives the bell another tug, grins at her, and is off.* ANNIE *gazes after him.*)

HELEN: Bed.

(ANNIE *stops her from leaving.*)

ANNIE [V.O.]: Trigonometry.

HELEN: Oh, no. Still?

ANNIE [V.O.]: Alas.

HELEN: I can't. I'll get up early—

ANNIE [V.O.]: Trig.

HELEN: I'm sleepy.

ANNIE [V.O.]: I'm comatose, don't argue!

(*This is a spat.* HELEN *offended trudges across to sit at her desk, bangs down stiletto, ruler, compass, and starts laboriously pricking out a diagram on stiff paper.*)

(ANNIE *gets a shopping bag, kneels with some short curtain rods on the floor.*)

HELEN [SITTING]: Carving out, one diagram, takes me all night. Do you, care?

ANNIE [LAYING OUT RODS]: Of course not.

HELEN [WORKING WITH THE STILETTO]: Jab, jab, jab—

(ANNIE *comes, spells.*)

ANNIE [V.O.]: Am I a slave driver?

HELEN: Yes.

ANNIE [V.O.]: You forgive me?

HELEN: Can I, go to bed?

ANNIE [V.O.]: No.

HELEN: No.

ANNIE [V.O.]: Here, I've invented something better.

(HELEN *kneels as* ANNIE *dumps out a box of child's blocks with raised letters.* HELEN *feels, starts up in disgust.*)

HELEN: Blocks!

ANNIE [V.O.]: Letters.

(*She slides a rod in* HELEN'S *fingers, in and out.*)

Lines.

HELEN: Ah. Why, didn't I, think of this?

ANNIE: *You* are not Euclid.

(*She gets a trig volume, sits to spell it to* HELEN, *V.O.*)

Raise a perpendicular from A to intersect OP—at point T—then AT is the tangent—

HELEN: Oh, trig is, boring!

(ANNIE *takes her hand;* HELEN *now lip-reads.*)

ANNIE: I never wanted to go to college, you did.

HELEN: I, do!

ANNIE: So.

HELEN: My youth is, withering on the, vine.

ANNIE [PAUSE]: Is it. Is it indeed—

(She means herself.)

At point B construct a line at right angles to BB prime—

(HELEN *places a rod as lights fade.*)

(Daylight up outside on doorbell area as JOHN *and a young man* PETE *walk in;* JOHN *is scanning a page of typescript,* PETE *holds a fat bundle of letters. They stand,* JOHN *reading.*)

JOHN: It's fine, Pete. Good article. Show it to our great white editor.

PETE: Will you talk to our great white editor?

JOHN: And say what?

PETE: Tell him I'm not an office boy.

JOHN: You are.

PETE: I'm a junior editor—leave my gorgeous adjectives in.

JOHN: Look, it's his magazine, you're a feudal serf. Go write a sonnet sequence, no one will edit you.

PETE: No one will pay me either. And tell him I'm worth two dollars more a week.

JOHN: I'll try for two adjectives. Give me the letters.

PETE [SEES THE CLOTHESLINE]: Helen Keller's *underwear?*

JOHN: She has all the usual plumbing.

PETE: Why can't I come in?

JOHN: Because you're not invited and I already have one battle on today's agenda.

PETE: I'll help you.

JOHN: Don't push, Pete. On your way.

PETE: You're a hog.

JOHN: No adjectives?

(Lights up inside; HELEN on a divan opposite an elderly gentleman ED on a chair, between them a checkerboard with sunken squares. PETE drifts off as JOHN comes into the room, puts the letters down.)

HELEN: Jump, Doctor Ed.

ED: How are things on the *Youth's Companion?*

JOHN: Immature. How are things in geriatrics?

ED: Senile.

(HELEN *jumps twice.)*

HELEN: King, me.

ED: Dammit.

JOHN: I need your help, doctor, you're an old friend of the girls—

ED [SITS A PIN INTO THE CHECKER]: Need a bit myself; on what?

JOHN: *Ladies Home Journal* gave them three thousand for the articles; there's a book in them—a significant book, will change teaching in this country if educators have any sense—

ED: Is a house interested?

JOHN: Doubleday. I proposed adding a hundred letters, beginning with Helen's first—

ED: Difficult to chase down.

JOHN: I've done it; the difficulty is with her teacher's. I have all Annie wrote that first year—two or three a week—

ED: Revenge.

(He jumps; ANNIE comes in with a tray of milk and sandwiches.)

JOHN: I think of her teacher's letters as the meat of the book.

HELEN [TO ED]: You have, a dismal, character.

ED: I do.

JOHN: And she won't let me use them.

ANNIE: *You* have a dismal character!—

ED [TO JOHN]: Why?

ANNIE: —behind my back?

JOHN: Doesn't want herself in it. I don't know why.

ED: Teacher, this is—

(HELEN *jumps twice.*)

—preposterous.

ANNIE [WARNING]: John, it's not debatable here.

JOHN: Then where?

ED: I surrender.

JOHN: You *are* in the articles.

ANNIE: Helen put me in.

JOHN: Leave you out she wouldn't have a word to write.

ED: Why is Johnny's proposal so distasteful?—it fills in a gap—

ANNIE [TURNS]: *You* know how we suffered with publicity.

ED: The public hardly knows you exist.

ANNIE: Good, I don't believe our affairs concern the public. Change the subject, please.

JOHN: Why won't she discuss it rationally?

ANNIE: Because I won't, we are on a different subject—

(*She sits beside* HELEN, *spelling.*)

—and Doctor Ed will tell us what he saw in the woods on his delightful walk this morning.

ED: Nothing much.

ANNIE [SPELLING]: Nothing much.

JOHN: Delightful subject. Can we get back to—

HELEN: I will tell, what he saw. A golden wheel, the sun rising back, of the dark hills asleep, waking the birds in the, woods to sing, don't say, nothing much.

ED: And she beats me at checkers too. If you have Helen you don't need a tonic.

(ANNIE *gets up abruptly.*)

JOHN: How does she know such things?

ED: Through her fingers, it's her genius to see into what we—

JOHN: There are no optic nerves in the fingers, doctor, she knows from her teacher.

ED: Of course.

JOHN: Who's found a principle of teaching that elicits her genius; it must be made known.

ED: Johnny is quite right, my dear, you owe it to the public.

ANNIE [BACK WITH A PLATE]: I won't lift a finger to enlighten the public on anything we've done, are doing, or intend to do; I will not discuss this further.

JOHN: You owe it to other teachers.

ED: You owe it to other children, deaf, blind—

JOHN: —To everyone who's victimized by hack teaching in—

ANNIE: I said I will not discuss this further!

(*She bangs her plate down, jumps up, and marches off; only* HELEN *is not startled.*)

HELEN: Teacher is in, one of her, moods.

(*Lights die as* JOHN *walks after* ANNIE *to the clothesline area.*)

JOHN: My, you're a contrary type; if you ever drown I'll look for you *up*stream.

ANNIE: I won't oblige. Go away.

JOHN: Why won't you talk to me?

ANNIE: Because you're too young.

JOHN: Why are you furious?

ANNIE: I'm not furious!

JOHN: Why are you not furious?

ANNIE: I'm just not delighted with people who look at me, and see Helen's faithful crutch, and prattle of her genius.

JOHN [PAUSE]: Ah.

ANNIE: I detest that word.

JOHN: I was quoting the good doctor. Look, Helen's chapters are charming; your letters are the most extraordinary account in the history of teaching, why be so damned modest?

ANNIE: Modest.

JOHN: I'm *determined* to get you into print.

ANNIE: What you don't know about me would fill another book.

JOHN: Tell me; I'll write that one.

ANNIE: I was nothing, till I found Helen. And that—love flooded me, what more could the world offer? Well, it offered all the grief of success. They couldn't keep their hands off her, do you know her father wanted to exhibit her for money?

JOHN: No—

ANNIE: Publicity. Do you know the Perkins teachers were so jealous of me they tried *her* for plagiarism?—and the Cambridge School thought she was such a feather in their cap they threw *me* out? I've been rescuing her most of her life, against all comers, and I'm sick to death of publicity.

JOHN: And—a bit jealous. From the background.

ANNIE: Of course. I've lived in her shadow for fifteen years, and for ten I've kept quiet.

JOHN: Why?

ANNIE: Because I have a mouthful of boils! I'm not your lovable angel of mercy, speak my mind and people can't stand me—men!—you think I'm modest? Do you know how avid I was for

praise and fame? I sit in class spelling every word those learned
spongeheads say, there aren't ten teachers in the country who
belong in a room with me and I've kicked the door open for the
other nine; I know that!

JOHN: That's all I want the book to say.

ANNIE: The book won't help.

JOHN: It will earn praise and fame for both of us; I'm avid too.
Fame isn't evil, it means people know you for what you are.

ANNIE: Don't equate us; what I am now is a female thirty-six years
old.

JOHN: Seven.

ANNIE [SITS]: Six till Tuesday.

JOHN: And act like a child.

ANNIE: I was never a child. You want my secret with Helen?—I
grew up in a garbage pail called the state poorhouse, with lunatics and syphilitic whores, and battled my way out, and I didn't
teach Helen, I *played* with her, games, games, games, her childhood was mine. A—garden. And all the time I knew that to
bring her into the light would make my life.

JOHN: And it isn't enough.

ANNIE: No. Not—enough—

(She suddenly scrambles up to escape, JOHN *catches her by the
ankle; she goes down, kicking.)*

Let go.

JOHN: No.

ANNIE: Let go!

(He pins her striking hands, kneels over her—)

JOHN: What would *be* enough?—A man who—

*(—and she knees him in the groin; he rolls over in pain. She
kneels.)*

ANNIE: Are you all right?

JOHN [GASPING]: You spit at me in public, you emasculate me in private, what is this feeling you have for me?

ANNIE: I don't know.

JOHN: Desist.

ANNIE: I never had it before.

(She kisses his mouth; waits over him, troubled.)

JOHN: Who taught you to kiss, the state poorhouse?

ANNIE: Nobody.

JOHN: Open your mouth.

(He reaches up, and they kiss; she comes out of it wide-eyed.)

ANNIE: Is that sanitary?

(JOHN whoops, rolls her over, and they kiss again, at length.)

Who taught you?

JOHN: Harvard.

ANNIE: It—deserves its reputation—

(Lights fade as they kiss.)

(Music now, as time passes—several months—)

(and when the lights slowly rise indoors they find HELEN in nightgown and wrapper in a rocker reading a Braille volume with her fingertips. JOHN steps in to the doorbell area, and tugs the bell; he has a bulky envelope.)

JOHN: Annie?

ANNIE [CALLS DOWN]: I'll be right down.

JOHN [CALLS UP]: I have the galleys.

(He drops the envelope on the floor, drapes his jacket around the chair at the desk, and kneels to lay out a floor display of the top galley sheets; this brings him a glimpse of HELEN, *and he walks over, places his hand on hers.)*

HELEN [SMILES]: John, dear.

JOHN [V.O.]: What's this, now?

HELEN [FINGERING IT]: "Prosperity, doth best discover, vice, but adversity, doth best discover, virtue." Who?

JOHN [V.O.]: Shakespeare.

HELEN [GLEEFUL]: Bacon. I win, for once.

(JOHN kisses her hand, for lip-reading—)

JOHN: No. Bacon wrote Shakespeare.

(—and kisses her brow. ANNIE *descends the steps to this sight, stops.)*

ANNIE: Am I interrupting?

JOHN: No, what? Oh. The supply is unlimited.

(He goes to kiss her mouth.)

HELEN [BAFFLED]: Bacon, wrote Shakespeare?

(JOHN returns to her, spells.)

JOHN [V.O.]: A theory, I'll bring the book. Come look at yours.

(She rises, leaving the volume in the rocker, and JOHN aims her.)

HELEN [WALKING]: And who, wrote Bacon? Shakespeare?

(ANNIE stops HELEN from walking on the galley sheets.)

ANNIE: *Warn* her of changes.

JOHN: Yes, ma'am.

ANNIE: Move a toothbrush, she can lose hours groping.

JOHN: I'll warn Pete tomorrow, don't use her toothbrush.

ANNIE: Strangers do move things.

JOHN: I'm not a stranger!—stop growling, you mick, I laid out a delightful vision, thank me. Next time I'll hit her hello.

(ANNIE *kneels with* HELEN, *guides her hand to the galley sheets;* JOHN *squats.)*

ANNIE [SOFTENING]: Thank you. It is.

JOHN [POINTS]: Title page.

(ANNIE *spells to* HELEN *throughout.)*

The Story of My Life, by Helen Keller. With a Supplementary Account of Her Education by John Albert Macy. Including Letters of Her Teacher, Anne Mansfield Sullivan.

HELEN: By Francis, Bacon.

ANNIE: Letters of her teacher, who may live to regret it.

JOHN: If you have faith you can move mountains; I did.

ANNIE: It's like taking off my clothes in Harvard Square.

JOHN: I hope to get them off somewhere.

(ANNIE *erases this midway from* HELEN'S *palm.)*

HELEN: What?

JOHN: "Chapter One. It is with a kind of fear that I begin to write the history of my life."

HELEN: The page, is longer than, my life.

JOHN: They cut them in half. Bind them, sell them everywhere, and make us rich. I drove a pitiless bargain.

(HELEN *reaches out—)*

HELEN: We are, rich. We have, each other.

(—and kisses both their hands.)

ANNIE [V.O.]: And a lovely child of a book. Thanks to John; no one else could have done it.

HELEN: John is in, dispensable.

JOHN: Brilliant.

ANNIE: Unique.

(She touches his face; they are lost in each other's eyes.)

HELEN: Read me, more.

ANNIE [V.O.]: Tomorrow.

HELEN: I must learn, what happened in my, life.

ANNIE [V.O.]: You lived. We have a long day tomorrow, and John's friend for supper. Off to bed, baby.

HELEN: No! While John, is here?

ANNIE [V.O.]: John is leaving.

JOHN [TAKES HIS CUE]: Yes, I'm just leaving.

(He kisses HELEN's cheek, ANNIE spelling.)

Good night, sleep tight, don't let the—

HELEN: I'm a grown woman.

JOHN: —flights of angels sing thee to thy rest.

HELEN: That's better.

(JOHN backs off, turns up the steps, and sits on ANNIE's bed; he takes off his shoes.)

I want to, discuss—

ANNIE [V.O.]: Helen, please go to bed!

(HELEN lifts her hand, to lip-read.)

WILLIAM CONVERSE-ROBERTS, KAREN ALLEN and JANE ALEXANDER

ANNIE: We read palms, faces —
HELEN: He is, talented.
JOHN: Thank you.
HELEN: And, knows it.

WILLIAM CONVERSE-ROBERTS and JANE ALEXANDER

JOHN: Who taught you to kiss, the state poorhouse?...
ANNIE: Who taught you?
JOHN: Harvard.
ANNIE: It — deserves its reputation.

WILLIAM CONVERSE-ROBERTS and KAREN ALLEN

HELEN: . . . when I feel, sculpture I think, Teacher hewed me, bit by bit out of the, dark like a face out of, stone.
JOHN: (V.O.): That's lovely.
HELEN: It seems, ungrateful for the, face to complain of, the chisel.
JOHN (V.O.): But are you stone?

WILLIAM CONVERSE-ROBERTS, JANE ALEXANDER and KAREN ALLEN

JOHN: Love. John loves Teacher. Teacher loves Helen. Helen and Teacher love John, and John loves Helen and Teacher. John and Helen and Teacher are one huge love-turd....

Photo credits: William Struhs

HELEN: Did he, go?

ANNIE: Yes.

HELEN: My eye, hurts.

ANNIE: Oh. Perhaps a crack in the glass; we may need a new eye. We'll visit the lab.

HELEN: Or consult, Doctor Ed. Tomorrow?

ANNIE: Yes. Sleep well—

(HELEN *kisses her, turns to grope her way up the steps,* ANNIE *watching.*)

—dear heart.

(ANNIE *gathers the galley sheets, then rises in fading light, and puts them on the chair with* JOHN'S *jacket. Stands troubled.*)

(*Lights up on* HELEN'S *bed as she works her artificial eyes out, and sets them in a glass of fluid.*)

(*Lights up on* ANNIE'S *bed as she goes upstairs, closes the imaginary door to her room, and leans against it.* JOHN, *lying on the bed, invites her with a hand.*)

JOHN: Come here.

(ANNIE *moves into* JOHN'S *arms.*)

(*Presently* HELEN *remembers, and in her nightgown makes her way down the steps in the dark; at the bottom she suddenly hesitates, to sniff. Sniffs again. She gropes toward her desk, and there finds* JOHN'S *jacket draped around the chair. And the galley sheets. She stands, pondering.*)

(*Then gropes to her rocker, to the Braille volume; she takes it with her up the steps. At the top she hesitates again, turns toward* ANNIE'S *bedroom, and rests her fingertips upon the imaginary door; she is listening.*)

(ANNIE *twists out of* JOHN'S *arms, shushing him; she rolls to sit on the edge of the bed, listens.* JOHN *reaches for her, she stops him with a hand.*)

(HELEN *after a moment goes back to her own bed, crawls in. Lights lose her.*)

(ANNIE *rises, stands at her own door.*)

ANNIE: She's gone.

JOHN: Come back.

ANNIE [DOESN'T]: I feel like a thief.

JOHN: Oh, God.

ANNIE: I think this has to stop, John.

JOHN: "This"?—is like teenagers, how old did you say you were, seven?

ANNIE: A hundred and seven. And ashamed to—be so—

JOHN: Human.

ANNIE: Osculatory. From Helen's geometry, touching at three points. I think of nothing but you now; I don't like you for it.

JOHN: Come touch me at three points.

ANNIE: Which I don't mind; I do mind disliking Helen. I'm cross with her every minute I want to be with you. And every minute with you I steal.

JOHN: Your time is not Helen's birthright.

ANNIE: Not only steal; when I disconnect from her I feel—weak, jumpy, something's missing I—Don't.

(JOHN *is behind her, kissing her nape, a hand on her bodice.*)

I feel miserable.

JOHN: Not to me.

ANNIE: And I have to get up at six-thirty.

(After a moment JOHN *drops his hands; he goes back to the bed to put on one shoe, hunts under it for the other.)*

JOHN: I've lost a shoe, as well as the lady.

ANNIE: I don't think we should see you again.

*(*JOHN *rises, shoe in hand, and stares.)*

JOHN: We? I don't come here to see Helen.

ANNIE: Are we sure?

JOHN: I'll be damned, you're still jealous.

ANNIE : I'm everything!—but do have eyes, the world beats a path through me to Helen, why are you different? I was clearheaded and single-minded till you began showering me with compliments and Karl Marx, I can't *read* those books! My job is to read Helen's; I'm a machine for spelling out Greek and Latin words, don't ask a machine to have feelings!

JOHN: As a machine you're inadequate.

ANNIE: I was adequate without you.

(She sits averted on the bed, shielding her face.)

And liked myself better. Oh, John. Please go away.

JOHN: You mean it.

ANNIE: Yes.

JOHN: You're firing me?

*(*ANNIE *is silent.)*

Now the book's done?—you still need an editor, your thinking is muddy.

ANNIE: Just go.

JOHN: May I put my shoe on first?

(He does.)

Goodbye forever?

(*After a moment he goes to the door, stops.*)

Good old Bridget.

ANNIE [IN HER HAND]: I prefer Maisie.

JOHN: How about Saint Joan? Listen—

(*He takes a breath.*)

Will you marry me?

(ANNIE *sits rigid.*)

Did you hear me?

ANNIE: Yes.

JOHN: Is that your answer?

ANNIE: No.

JOHN: Is that your answer?

ANNIE: John. You're twenty-six years old; I'm not certain what we're talking about; please go and—

JOHN: Love; you've heard of it?

ANNIE: No. I'm not—

JOHN: It makes the world go round. I think of nothing but you and I do like you for it—

ANNIE: —not so lovable. I—

JOHN: —and I want to be with you days, nights, Saturdays and Sundays—Karl Marx and Pestalozzi's birthdays—

ANNIE: I think you're in love with affliction.

JOHN: True, not pertinent.

ANNIE: And in this house the affliction is—forgive me—famous around the world; you're young, and suggestible, and—

JOHN: Tell me what you feel.

ANNIE: I don't know what I feel!

JOHN: Then don't tell me what I feel. Will you marry me?

ANNIE: I can't marry!

JOHN [PAUSE]: Try sleeping on it. Till six-thirty. I'll come to-morrow.

ANNIE: No.

JOHN: With Pete, for supper.

ANNIE: No.

JOHN: Southern-fried chicken, please, we'll be here at seven.

ANNIE: I'm married to Helen!

JOHN: How many children are you planning on?

(He goes out, and down the steps in the dark, picks up the galley sheets and his jacket, and leaves.)

(ANNIE sits still; but her thoughts move, her hand comes down to her abdomen.)

(Lights out on her. Voices offstage.)

PETE [OFFSTAGE]: A doll's house.

JOHN [OFFSTAGE]: It's handy for Radcliffe; they talk of moving afterwards. They want country—

PETE: —birds, bees—

JOHN: —mosquitoes, snakes—

(Lights up as he tugs at the bell; he has a bottle of bourbon.)

—where they'll feel at home, one's a tiger, one's a flower. You'll like them.

(He ushers PETE in, lights now including the lower areas as PETE gazes around, stops at HELEN'S desk.)

(ANNIE is seated on HELEN'S bed with her.)

HELEN: Do you, kiss?

ANNIE [V.O.]: Yes.

HELEN: What else?

ANNIE [V.O.]: Touch.

HELEN: You do, everything?

ANNIE [V.O.]: No.

HELEN [BITTER]: Why not?

ANNIE [V.O.]: It's not a—promise I'm ready to make—

HELEN: I thought he, liked *me*.

ANNIE: Ohhh—baby—

(ANNIE *on the point of tears tightens her clasp on* HELEN'S *hand.*)

(JOHN *brings in a casserole.*)

JOHN: I said fried, she doesn't take orders gracefully.

(PETE *dips a finger in, licks it.*)

PETE: Smart woman.

JOHN: Oh, she can cook.

(*He opens the bourbon.*)

Have a chair.

PETE: That's her Braille machine?

(JOHN *nods,* PETE *lays his bouquet on it.*)

What's keeping them?

JOHN: God knows.

PETE: Well, here's to.

(They drink.)

(ANNIE *comes down the steps, grim; the men watch as without a word she ladles food onto a plate, catches up silverware—*)

JOHN: This is Pete.

ANNIE: Goodbye, Pete.

(—and carries it all out, up the steps to HELEN'S *bedroom.)*

PETE: I like them.

(JOHN *downs his drink, goes after* ANNIE.)

(ANNIE *gives* HELEN *the plate, turns out to intercept* JOHN *outside the room.)*

ANNIE: She knows, she doesn't want to see you.

(They stand a moment; then ANNIE *kisses him, and goes back in, closing the imaginary door.)*

JOHN: Oh, Christ.

(He half descends.)

PETE: Was that the flower?

JOHN [WHEELS]: No.

PETE: Thank God.

(JOHN *back at the door opens it, invades* HELEN'S *room.)*

JOHN: She *is* going to see me. Why did you tell her, blabber-mouth?

ANNIE: I didn't.

JOHN: Why not, ashamed of me?

(He sits beside HELEN, *takes her hand; she pulls back. He opens her fist, spells.)*

Did, I, hurt, you?

ANNIE: Don't.

HELEN: Yes.

JOHN [V.O.]: I hurt with you. Because I care for you, I feel what you feel.

HELEN: I don't, believe you.

JOHN [V.O.]: Do you love Teacher?

HELEN: In, ordinately.

JOHN [V.O.]: So do I. You mustn't—

HELEN: Then, tell her.

JOHN [V.O.]: —feel *un*loved, because part of that is you, her work in you. I am proud of her work. I love you too, as she does—

HELEN [STANDS]: No, more! Must I, dine in the, closet?

(She gropes down the steps, where PETE *sees her.)*

ANNIE: You're making things worse.

JOHN: Did you mention marriage?

ANNIE: Of course not.

JOHN: It's ridiculous, I come here to woo you and have to woo her first?

ANNIE: I said don't come.

PETE: You are the flower.

JOHN [RISES]: I won't, dammit!

ANNIE: I shatter her picture of me, you step on her heart, we leave her alone and terrified, and you think a word from you is the cure? I need *days* with her—

JOHN: Take six months; I'll be back when asked and not before!

ANNIE: John—

(She follows as JOHN *stomps down the steps, picks up the bourbon.)*

JOHN: Women! Marry them both?

PETE: I'll help—

*(*JOHN *tugs the doorbell violently, and they walk off.)*

ANNIE [V.O.]: He's gone.

HELEN: That is what you said last night.

ANNIE [V.O.]: I wanted some—privacy—

HELEN [PULLING]: So do I.

ANNIE [V.O.] [EXASPERATED]: I'm not allowed to have an admirer?

HELEN: You never did.

ANNIE [V.O.]: That's a silly and selfish—

HELEN: You're not allowed to, lie to me!

ANNIE [V.O.]: That's different. I—

HELEN: I don't want, him in this house.

ANNIE [V.O.]: It's mine too.

HELEN: In my half! He changes, everything be, tween us.

ANNIE [V.O.]: No. Nothing is—

HELEN: Then why, did you lie?

ANNIE [V.O.]: Because I'm not allowed an admirer!

HELEN: Did I, say that?

ANNIE [V.O.]: I said it!

HELEN: Then you, answer it.

(She pulls away, gropes out. ANNIE *stands alone.)*

ANNIE: Because *I* think I'm not.

(Music; she goes to the top step, sits while in the dark the set is cleared below. And begins improvising a letter.)

Dear John. Johnny dearest. I'm asking you to—join us Sunday. To look at the house for sale in Wrentham. Helen will be happy to have you. Or I'll throttle her.

(She steps outside, where JOHN *waits to wrap a coat around her.)*

You can't understand how the past—picks at me—

JOHN: Ho.

ANNIE: —you're too young to have one.

JOHN: It's a dead hand; welcome to the twentieth century, *everything* new. Give us fifty years, we'll sweep this old world clean.

ANNIE: Nothing's new. I thought I solved the problem of my life, with Helen; now she's the problem.

JOHN: I keep saying I'm the answer, nobody listens.

(They are crossing front to the area formerly for clothesline; ED *and* HELEN *in coats wait here. The set is now bare except for a broken chair on an upper platform.)*

ED [V.O.]: Well, here's the house, ample enough. Been empty for a year, I believe you can get it for a song.

HELEN: I don't, sing. It smells like, heaven here. Pines?

ED [V.O.]: Pines. Come.

(He leads HELEN *into the set.* ANNIE *turns for* JOHN, *who is plucking at a clump of white-pine needles.)*

JOHN: Yes, no, yes, no—

(He shows one needle left.)

Yes.

ANNIE: You know it has five.

JOHN: Nature doesn't lie, she loves and will marry me.

ANNIE [NOT HAPPILY]: She loves.

(She turns to follow HELEN in.)

ED: Needs paint, of course. I love this space—

JOHN: I can run ropelines all along those pines, she'll have a walk.

ED: And there's a handsome bedroom with balcony upstairs—

(He turns HELEN toward the steps, ANNIE and JOHN following.)

HELEN: We have the, stocks Mr. Spaulding, left us—

ANNIE: It's our nest egg.

JOHN: Here's the nest, you put the egg into it.

(He takes HELEN'S hand, spells V.O.)

I can do wonders with this place, I'm very handy—

HELEN: I said, come. Not, converse.

(She gropes up, ED coming back grasps her hand; they go out on a platform.)

ANNIE: I'm eleven years older.

ED [V.O.]: This could be your bedroom—

JOHN: I'm very juvenile, I need mothering.

HELEN [FACE UPLIFTED]: Oh, the sun.

(ED and HELEN go out. JOHN and ANNIE mount the platform.)

ANNIE: You don't know me yet.

JOHN: I think you're a great mother.

ANNIE: Mother isn't wife. I'm detestable, bossy, full of distrust and

contempt, I find most people hateful and I hate them, I've had—
arson in my heart as long as I can remember—

JOHN: Well, I won't put up with any of that. I'm perfect.

ANNIE: I think that—would be necessary—

JOHN: And this would make a perfect nursery.

(ANNIE *breaks from him, walks, shakes her head.*)

ANNIE: You're wicked.

JOHN: Too.

ANNIE: I want children, oh, I want children.

JOHN: Here I am.

ANNIE: And the time is short.

JOHN: So.

ANNIE: You don't see, she and I—

JOHN: I do.

ANNIE: —are sharing one life—

JOHN: Look, I promise you a different life. In which *you* are nur-
tured. Taught, cherished, opened up, body and mind, in every
way spinsterhood is leaving you arid.

(*Long pause.*)

ANNIE: I can't *leave* her.

JOHN: I won't ask that. I want you, any way it—

ANNIE: With her?

JOHN: I can handle it.

(*They are negotiating a bargain for life; now* ANNIE *ponders.*)

ANNIE: I want her consent.

JOHN: Tell her.

ANNIE: You tell her.

(JOHN *hesitates, flutters his hands in fear, and sits on the chair.*)

JOHN: That will require some thought.

(*The chair breaks under him; dumped on the floor, he stays, mock collapsed, and* ANNIE *comes to kneel.*)

ANNIE: You shouldn't think so *hard;* we'll both tell her.

(JOHN *rolls her over in an embrace;* ED *guides* HELEN *back in, below.*)

JOHN: When?

ANNIE: Now.

HELEN: It feels like, a happy house.

ED [CALLS]: Teacher?

HELEN: If she, likes it too—

ANNIE [CALLS]: Here.

HELEN: —I think, we can, purchase it.

ANNIE: Let me up.

JOHN: Never. No knees now, it's joint property.

ED [CALLS]: I believe we have a buyer.

JOHN: Do I have a buyer?

ANNIE: Yes.

(JOHN *pulls her up; they separate.*)

JOHN: To it.

(ANNIE *descends first, takes* HELEN'S *hand.*)

ED: She likes it.

ANNIE: Good.

ED: And I like congenial neighbors—

ANNIE: I think Helen and I must talk.

ED: Of course you must. But I'll sound out—

ANNIE: Alone.

ED: Oh. Fine. Come along, Johnny.

(JOHN *is tempted*—)

ANNIE: You wait.

(—*and he stops.* ED *peers at them.*)

ED: Oho. Are congratulations in order?

(*He waits, neither answers.*)

I'm out of order. Not Ida; lunch is at one, and Ida is strict.

(*He ambles off.*)

ANNIE [V.O.]: John has something to say to you.

HELEN: No.

ANNIE [V.O.]: He's asked me to marry him, baby.

(HELEN *slips her hand free, stands; she has to digest this.*)

HELEN: What did, you answer?

(*She puts out her hand again;* JOHN *moves in to take it.*)

JOHN [V.O.]: She wants you to say yes.

HELEN: Are you proposing, to me?

JOHN [V.O.]: Helen—

ANNIE: Give her time.

HELEN: If not, it's not my, business. To say, anything.

JOHN [V.O.]: It seems to be. Teacher—

HELEN: You will allow us, to complete my, degree first?

ANNIE: God help us, yes, what kind of question is that?

(JOHN *spells it.*)

HELEN: Thank you.

(*She withdraws her hand, turns back a step or two.*)

JOHN: Your turn.

HELEN: It's ridiculous, Doctor Ed, to discuss, purchasing a house, now.

(*She puts her hand out—*)

Doctor Ed?

(*—and* ANNIE *moves to it quickly.*)

ANNIE [V.O.]: He's gone. You're misunderstanding—

HELEN: Gone?

ANNIE [V.O.]: —yes, misunderstanding us both. The—

HELEN: There's nobody, here?

ANNIE [V.O.]: Only John.

HELEN [A WAIL]: How can, you let him take, you from me?

(*She breaks away, blunders to her knees;* ANNIE *is after her, fights for her hand.*)

What am I, to do?—

JOHN: Oh, God.

HELEN: —go back to, Alabama?—and be a—

ANNIE [V.O.]: Listen—

HELEN: —cow?

ANNIE [V.O.]: Now listen to me.

HELEN: No!

ANNIE [V.O.]: You will decide.

HELEN: No—

JOHN: I withdraw my proposal to you, I do make it to her.

ANNIE: John, be quiet.

JOHN: She'll *decide?*—you said consent.

HELEN: What's to, become of me?

JOHN: What kind of mother lets a child make decisions on matters of—

ANNIE: Go outside!

JOHN: You said stay.

ANNIE: Stay and help, or go outside; I don't need nonsense.

JOHN: I'll help.

ANNIE [V.O.]: You're worse than a cow, you're a stupid piglet.

HELEN: I may be, selfish; I'm not stupid.

ANNIE [V.O.]: You are, to think John and I would send you to Alabama. You would live with us.

HELEN: No.

JOHN: Or *he* will.

(ANNIE *gives him a look.*)

I'm helping!

ANNIE [V.O.]: Or, *he* will.

HELEN: I don't, *want* him.

ANNIE [V.O.]: Three instead of two. And whatever we do for a lifework, I get a helper in it.

JOHN: Good point.

ANNIE [V.O.]: Because John is perfect.

HELEN: No.

ANNIE [V.O.]: For us. With a passion for breaking the world's chains; who would be more loving of the work I do with you?

HELEN: He's, my age.

ANNIE [V.O.]: Very true. And when I—retire, at a hundred and eight, I'll be leaving you in good hands. I won't live forever.

HELEN: Don't, say that.

ANNIE: I think it. And I won't find a better third.

JOHN: She has to earn a living, by writing—

ANNIE: She knows that.

JOHN: —tell her I can help there too.

ANNIE: Yes.

(She spells it.)

Nothing will change, except for the better—

HELEN: Are you, marrying just for, my sake?

JOHN: Not quite.

HELEN: All these reasons are, nothing. I don't need a, better third.

ANNIE: I do.

HELEN: *Why?*

(A pause.)

ANNIE [V.O.]: I want love. His. I want children. Of my own. I'm thirty-seven. I want—a life, as a woman.

(HELEN gets up, leaving ANNIE; moves a blind step, here and there; stands. And finally turns.)

HELEN: You must be, married in, this house.

(JOHN comes to squeeze her hand; ANNIE comes to her also; and JOHN puts his arms around both, binding them in a threesome.)

ACT TWO

ACT II

SET DARK.

A CRACK OF LIGHT, AS THROUGH CURTAINS, STEALS IN ON UPPER PLATFORM; BARELY VISIBLE, ANNIE AND JOHN IN BED UNDER BLANKETS, ASLEEP.

AN ALARM CLOCK RINGS, RINGS.

JOHN: Oh God, kill it.

(ANNIE *reaches to turn it off; sinks back. Both half asleep.*)

What time is it?

ANNIE: Seven.

JOHN: Seven what?

ANNIE: O'clock.

JOHN: A.m.?

ANNIE: Don't.

JOHN: What?

ANNIE: Talk.

JOHN: What day is it?

ANNIE: Sunday.

JOHN: Sunday. I'll eat that clock, why?

ANNIE: Deadline. Helen has a deadline.

JOHN: Oh. Give her the clock. C'mere.

ANNIE [IN HIS ARMS]: Ummm.

JOHN: Took the word out of my mouth.

ANNIE: I like your arms.

JOHN: Let's.

ANNIE: I haven't the strength.

JOHN: Never said that the first year.

ANNIE: Don't grumble; you had us up till two.

JOHN: Well, it's habit-forming. Feel.

ANNIE: Hello.

JOHN: The first time you said how ingenious of God, are all men like that?

ANNIE: You lied.

JOHN: Who?

ANNIE: You said no, I'm the only one.

JOHN: Didn't want you—How do you know I lied?

ANNIE: Ida told me.

JOHN: No fooling, Ed too, eh? Open, sesame!

ANNIE: No, I'm—sore—

JOHN: Oh. A compliment.

(ANNIE *gets up, puts on a wrapper.*)

Come back, we'll talk.

ANNIE: Tonight. Up!—

(*She goes, as to a window—*)

—there's work to do—

(*—and flings imaginary curtains open to the sun; lights up, in other areas too.*)

JOHN [GROANING]: It's Sunday—

(This is the new house, a few years later; on the other platform is JOHN's *desk with typewriter, and downstairs an "office" with desk and couch and great piles of correspondence on both; in the outside area is a terrace table, where* HELEN *sits in the sun.)*

—the Lord's day of rest—

ANNIE [AT THE WINDOW]: He earned it; look what He created.

JOHN: Me. To loaf, and invite my soul.

(He sits up, in pajamas; gropes for slippers.)

But at my back I always hear / Time's winged chariot hurrying —up my sphincter—

(He makes for the other platform. ANNIE, *below, finds her dark glasses amid the correspondence, contemplates it all heavily; opens a letter to read—)*

ANNIE: Oh, God give us patience.

(—and takes a handful with her into a passageway behind left platform—an unseen kitchen.)

JOHN: Not unreasonable, once a week to luxuriate in bed among my beautiful thoughts—

(He reads the page in his typewriter.)

Pretty damn good, Macy, why don't your books sell? They will, they will! Give me leave / To speak my mind—

(Turns, comes down the steps as ANNIE *reappears outside with a tray—fruits and whatnot, plates, and the letters—to bring to* HELEN. JOHN *goes behind the platform;* ANNIE *sets three plates out, kisses* HELEN.)*

HELEN: There was a, bird. On the table. It sang.

*(*ANNIE *sits; they begin to eat.)*

The table, trilled.

ANNIE [NOT SPELLING]: So did the alarm clock.

[v.o.]: There's an urgent letter you must rush to answer.

HELEN: From whom?

ANNIE [V.O.]: A fascinating schoolgirl.

HELEN: I will.

ANNIE [V.O.]: "I wonder what you are doing today. I am not doing anything much—"

HELEN: We must, send her a, telegram.

ANNIE [NOT SPELLING]: Collect.

(ANNIE *opens other letters.* HELEN'S *plate is not empty, but she mischievously sneaks a hand out to* ANNIE'S—)

JOHN [COMING OUT]: The god Thor dropped out of the clouds onto a peachy milkmaid; when done—

(—*and* ANNIE *slaps it; they giggle; then* ANNIE *holding* HELEN'S *hand looks up to see* JOHN *standing with coffeepot and mugs.*)

ANNIE: Oh, John, don't look like that.

JOHN: How?

ANNIE: Glum. It's an old joke, the first time I ate with Helen—

JOHN: I got the joke, I edited the spelling in those letters.

ANNIE: I beg your pardon. I thought you were feeling—

(HELEN *waggles her hand for the conversation;* ANNIE *spells V.O.*)

Nothing. Coffee.

(JOHN *pours;* ANNIE *finishes to him.*)

—left out.

JOHN: Just telling another old joke.

ANNIE [POURS FOR HELEN]: What?

JOHN: He said, I am Thor. She said, You're Thor, how do you thuppothe I—

HELEN: The air is, idyllic.

JOHN: I think *Helen* feels left out.

HELEN: Must we slave, indoors?

ANNIE [V.O.]: We have a deadline.

HELEN: Let's slave, outdoors.

ANNIE [V.O.]: No.

JOHN: What do you say to *The Spirit of American Literature?*

ANNIE: Hooray.

JOHN: For a title!— *The Spirit of American Literature,* the best critique ever, by John Macy, the well known prophet. Give me leave / To speak my mind, and I will through and through / Cleanse the foul body of th'infected world—

ANNIE: Did you write that?

JOHN: You like it?

ANNIE: Yes.

JOHN: It's called *As You Like It.* Let's have a picnic today.

ANNIE: No. You have your work, we have ours—

JOHN: I invited Pete. For Helen.

ANNIE: What?

JOHN: He's visiting friends.

(Spells to HELEN'S *hand, V.O.)*

Shall we have a picnic, in honor of my new chapter?

HELEN: Mar, velous.

JOHN [V.O.]: At the lake. With Pete.

HELEN: And, swim!

JOHN: The ayes have it.

ANNIE: Who feels left out?

JOHN: That's democracy.

ANNIE: I never voted for democracy. We'll work.

JOHN: Voted for implies what you think you're rejecting. See how the system infects language?—*and* the process of thought; you embrace bourgeois parliamentarianism in the act of spurning it.

ANNIE: The things you bring into our lives!—Marx, Shakespeare, Joe Miller's jokebook—

(Spells to HELEN, *V.O.)*

We'll still work. I'll be inside, the sun is too bright.

JOHN: What do I do with Pete?

ANNIE: Take him on a picnic.

(She takes letters and mug with her, goes behind the platform, reappears to head for the office.)

HELEN: I didn't, consider her, eyes.

JOHN [V.O.]: Maybe it will rain, for a picnic.

HELEN: No swim.

(ANNIE in the office is halted over another letter in hand.)

ANNIE: Letters, letters, letters. It's Noah's flood.

HELEN: But she's right. This week is, frantic; the state, commission meets and I, must testify.

JOHN [V.O.] [STOPS HER RISING]: What commission?

HELEN: For the blind. The governor, appointed me.

(She goes in, after ANNIE.)

JOHN [ALONE]: And she goes with you?

HELEN: I'm ready.

ANNIE: I'm not.

(ANNIE *looks around, remembers.*)

Yes.

HELEN: Saving the eyes of hundreds, of infants, will be more, lasting than a, picnic. Let's en, list John to, read.

(ANNIE *catches up a medical encyclopedia;* HELEN *sits on the office chair;* JOHN *passes through with a tumblerful of whiskey.*)

ANNIE: For breakfast?

JOHN: For company. Poe is driving me to drink—

ANNIE: Do Emerson.

JOHN: —or drink is driving me to Poe; either way we're stuck with each other.

ANNIE: Can I help?

JOHN: Just hold *my* hand, now and then.

ANNIE: The one with the drink?

JOHN: The one that's cold—

(He lays it on her bosom; she takes it to kiss, and goes to HELEN *with the encyclopedia;* JOHN *remains on the steps.)*

ANNIE: Now where were we, yes.

[v.o.]: "In gonorrheal births—"

HELEN: The book of, sacred love.

ANNIE [v.o.]: —"conjunctivitis in both eyes is frequently followed by ulceration of the cornea. The retrotarsal fold—"

HELEN: Retro?

(ANNIE *looks about, hauls a dictionary from the desk;* JOHN, *leaving the tumbler on a step, approaches;* ANNIE *thumbs through the dictionary—)*

ANNIE: Retrotarsal—

(—and pinches her eyelids, which hurt.)

JOHN: I'll spell you.

(He sits beside her, she surrenders the dictionary.)

ANNIE: She's doing the silver-nitrate article on venereal births—

JOHN: It's fuzzy, I did a new outline for you yesterday. Sharper.

ANNIE [GRATEFUL]: Oh, Johnny.

JOHN: You're welcome. They'll still run her out of Boston.

(He takes HELEN'S *hand.)*

HELEN: Good; we need more, eyes.

JOHN: Retrotarsal—

ANNIE [WITH THE ENCYCLOPEDIA]: Shall we see a doctor?

JOHN: About retrotarsal?—here—

ANNIE: About us. It's not flattering to think I'm—an empty vessel.

JOHN: Takes two to be empty. If not three.

ANNIE: What?

JOHN: If the womb doesn't want another child?—maybe it thinks Helen—

ANNIE: What?

JOHN: —is enough.

HELEN: Retro, something.

JOHN [V.O.]: Retro, back of. Tarsal—

ANNIE: Sorry I mentioned it.

JOHN [V.O.]: —eyelid tissue. Which—

ANNIE: Shall I write your book?

JOHN: What?

(ANNIE *takes the dictionary back.*)

You're reading yourself blind over this damned article.

ANNIE: Not in the next three hours; you have three hours before more nutrition.

JOHN [RISES]: Oh God, you're a captain of industry! When do you *play?*

(*He walks out, picks up the tumbler;* ANNIE *spells aloud to* HELEN *from the encyclopedia.*)

ANNIE [V.O.]: "The retrotarsal fold—"

HELEN: Where is, John?

ANNIE [V.O.]: "—in all newborn infants—"

(*She bites her tongue, shakes her head; rises to go after* JOHN. *He is on the top step.*)

I'm sorry I'm such a—despot. You complain about routine at the office, here's a day you can do your own book, and I don't want your work sacrificed to mine.

JOHN: It gets lonely.

ANNIE: So does mine.

JOHN: You have Helen Keller for company.

ANNIE: You have Edgar Allan Poe.

JOHN: Yes, he's jolly. The trouble with Poe—Can you spare a minute?

ANNIE: Yes.

JOHN: —is his *music*, where are my own poems?—unwritten. While I scribble about his.

ANNIE: No.

JOHN: What do you mean no?

ANNIE: Your gift is criticism.

JOHN: You don't like my poems?

ANNIE: I love your poems, go up and write me one.

JOHN: I need mouth-to-mouth resuscitation.

ANNIE: She's waiting, John. Now please go upstairs and—

JOHN: Come up with me.

   (Pause.)

   Come up with me.

ANNIE: I'm with you.

JOHN: No.

ANNIE: I'm downstairs in body, upstairs in spirit.

JOHN: That's a bad bargain. Can I say the same if I—

ANNIE: Go up to work! I'll buy a padlock for that door—

JOHN: So I won't feel left out? Why didn't you tell me the governor made her a commissioner?

ANNIE: I was—waiting—

JOHN: For what, you think I resent her honors?

ANNIE [SIMPLY]: Yes.

JOHN: It's the *time* I resent!

   (He goes up, with the tumbler, to his own typewriter; ANNIE stands looking after him.)

HELEN: Lovers. Lovers everywhere. And not a, drop to drink.

   (Outside, PETE comes in to the terrace table, eyes the dishes; he carries a beribboned box of candy.)

ANNIE: Why am I the Genghis Khan of this caravan?

(She makes for the steps.)

John!

JOHN: Yes?

ANNIE: Come downstairs.

(PETE hears. ANNIE goes back to spell V.O. to HELEN; JOHN begins down with the tumbler.)

We're going to the lake and revel in the beauties of nature.

HELEN: Not if, your eyes, hurt—

ANNIE: I'll keep them closed. Put a tablecloth and napkins in the hamper—

(PETE goes in, behind the platform.)

JOHN [IN]: Reporting from exile, duchess. What?

ANNIE: Duchess. Get dressed, I'm done giving orders. There's cold ham and wine in the icebox, make sandwiches.

JOHN: I'm—confused—

ANNIE: The suits are on the pantry rack; don't forget the oars. And bring *King Lear,* I need cheering up.

(Spells V.O. to HELEN.)

John will read us something immortal and explain it.

HELEN [HAPPILY]: Swedenborg.

JOHN: Swedenborg!—

ANNIE: Swedenborg, then.

JOHN: —I'd rather work.

HELEN: Who brings, God close.

JOHN: He's crazy!

ANNIE: Helen won't meet her deadline, you'll throw Poe in the wastebasket, and I'll enjoy life. But not make love in the row-boat—

(PETE *enters with the candy, is ignored;* HELEN *gropes out.)*

—because it hurts.

JOHN: What hurts?

ANNIE: Some—inflammation—

JOHN: Serious?

ANNIE: Minor. Where would she be if I weren't the ugly duchess? —and I don't have her instead of your baby, I have you. Be ready or I'll go alone.

(She goes up into the bedroom to change; JOHN *glowers at* PETE.)

PETE [SHOWS THE CANDY]: I—

JOHN: Swedenborg. I want *her!*

(He tromps upstairs, after ANNIE. PETE *is left alone, holding the candy.)*

PETE: This house is worse than the other—

(HELEN *comes in with tablecloth and napkins, to set down; senses* PETE, *stops.)*

HELEN: Who is, there?

PETE [V.O.]: Pete.

HELEN [PLEASED]: You are, spelling! More than, your name?

(PETE *takes a deep breath.)*

PETE [V.O.]: Helen, thy beauty is to me / Like those Nicean barks of yore—

HELEN: Oh?

PETE [V.O.]: That, gently o'er a perfumed sea / The weary, way-worn wanderer bore—

HELEN: Thank you.

(She pats his cheek; pauses on her way out.)

Do you, always speak in, rhyme?

(She goes out.)

PETE: I will from now on.

(Lights fade on him and the house.)

(Music, time passing.)

(And daylight up on the bedroom and stairs, as ED descends with his doctor's bag; at the couch he sets it down, stands scribbling a prescription. ANNIE appears above, buttoning up.)

ANNIE: I've been praying for offspring.

ED: It can't hurt.

ANNIE: Can't help, I'm a *retired* Catholic. Is it menstrual?

ED: No.

ANNIE: It's been irregular.

ED: No. Here, you can take this for the tiredness. No profuse flows?

ANNIE: Not now.

ED: I want to see you in the office, Teacher. Are you in town this week?

ANNIE: Wednesday.

ED: Four-thirty?—I'll squeeze you in—

ANNIE: Why?

ED: No mystery but we'll check it out. How old are you now?

ANNIE: Forty-two. The other day I was twenty-two.

(ED *is silent.*)

What is it?

ED: Uterine fibroids, I think.

ANNIE: Uterine—?

ED: Muscle-fibre tumor.

ANNIE: That sounds—seductive.

ED: Not uncommon in midlife.

ANNIE: Is that the trouble?

ED: Too many factors to say. I should see Johnny.

ANNIE: We're a little—desperate to have one—

ED: We'll do our best.

ANNIE: He does.

(ED *locks his bag; she walks him outside.*)

ED: I'm worried about that eye, I'd like Oscar to look at it.

ANNIE: I will not have another eye operation.

ED: You're over-using it; keep it up you'll lose what's left. Give it a good rest. A winter cruise—lie on a beach and bake—we'll take Helen off your hands—

ANNIE: Rest exhausts me.

ED: And get Johnny out of the house. It might make a difference.

ANNIE: How?

ED: I said might. Take your iron and I'll see you Wednesday.

ANNIE: Iron. I'll be adorable.

(She shows ED *out.)*

(Night in the house; only a footlight glow, as from a fireplace, in the office. JOHN *walks* HELEN *in, spelling.)*

JOHN [V.O.]: —and the two of them wrote—in the *Communist Manifesto*, 1847—all government is the executive committee of the ruling class.

HELEN: What a, phrase!

JOHN [V.O.]: And that opened up a vista on all history.

HELEN: Yes.

JOHN [V.O.]: The pieces fall into place; it's as esthetic as it is political.

HELEN: And, exciting.

JOHN [V.O.]: But not to her. She's a stiff-necked lady.

HELEN [LAUGHS]: Yes.

(They settle, belly down.)

I love Teacher. But—it's true, living with her, is like—

JOHN [V.O.]: Yes?

HELEN: Being in a, vise.

JOHN [V.O.]: On occasion.

HELEN: On, occasion. But when I feel, sculpture I think, Teacher hewed me, bit by bit out of the, dark like a face out of, stone.

JOHN [V.O.]: That's lovely.

HELEN: It seems, ungrateful for the, face to complain of, the chisel.

JOHN [V.O.]: But are you stone?

HELEN [LAUGHS]: Oh, many people, think I'm a, statue.

JOHN [V.O.]: Winged.

HELEN: With feet of, clay. Even now, if I type one, mistake she throws the page, back at me.

JOHN [V.O.]: You must understand, she's an artist; you're her art. She wants it flawless.

HELEN: I, try.

JOHN [V.O.]: Which relegates me to my art.

HELEN: Do I, usurp her?

JOHN [V.O.]: Obsess, I think. But it's what I love in her.

HELEN: Yes.

JOHN [V.O.]: On occasion.

HELEN: On, occasion?

JOHN [V.O.]: Alternate Tuesdays.

HELEN: And in, between?

JOHN [V.O.]: I wait.

HELEN: For her?

JOHN [V.O.]: For her art.

(HELEN *withdraws her palm.* JOHN *recaptures it to spell.*)

Don't hide; why are we here at the fire together?

HELEN: I'm, infatuated with the, smell of pine.

JOHN [V.O.]: Only pine?

HELEN: Some, hickory too.

JOHN [V.O.] Oh, you're perverse.

HELEN: But there's a, fascinating creature, with me.

JOHN [V.O.]: Good; continue.

HELEN: A, squirrel.

JOHN [V.O.]: Thank you. How do you know?

HELEN: Because I, listen.

(She puts his fingers to the floor.)

In the attic, there are baby, mice.

JOHN [V.O.]: How do you know that?

HELEN: I, smelled the nest and, found it. Little lives, no bigger than a, pinky tip.

JOHN [V.O.]: What other wild life is in the house?

HELEN: You.

(Pause.)

JOHN [V.O.]: Yes. I thought I was domesticated by now; it seems not.

(He pats her hand, starts to rise.)

HELEN: Don't go. Do you think I'm unaware of a, man in the house?—you are, everywhere.

JOHN [V.O.]: Tell me.

HELEN: The bathroom, seat up; I fall in.

JOHN [V.O.]: Oh, God. Forgive me.

HELEN: Suspenders, on the doorknob and the, smell of, your tobacco, and books I, don't know on, the stairs—

JOHN [V.O.]: I sound messy.

HELEN: —yes, equals man, and your shoes are, thumpier than the, squirrel's.

JOHN [V.O.]: That's brains.

HELEN: The house is alive with a, mystery. What is, man?

JOHN [V.O.]: That thou art mindful of him?

HELEN: Since you first, came. And my darkness was, spangled with unexpected, thoughts from a man's, hand. So much we didn't dream of. And not only, brains.

JOHN [V.O.]: No.

HELEN: Do you think I'm, reposeful in my, maidenly bed when next, door she lies in a man's, arms? And I am never to, know what that is, like?

JOHN [V.O.]: Why never?

HELEN: It is not, in the books.

JOHN [V.O.]: It's like—This.

(He turns her face, to kiss her on the lips.)

HELEN: How, curious. Am I, acceptable?

JOHN [V.O.]: Very.

(HELEN now spells; they converse by fingers, kissing, and we hear HELEN'S mind-voice, which is normal.)

HELEN [V.O.]: I will never speak to you again. Only spell.

JOHN [V.O.]: Why?

HELEN [V.O.]: My voice is ugly.

JOHN [V.O.]: No.

HELEN [V.O.]: My most dismal failure.

JOHN [V.O.]: Failure. You?

HELEN [V.O.]: Oh, in many things I fall short.

JOHN [V.O.]: Of what?

HELEN [V.O.]: Of what Teacher expects. This, now.

JOHN [V.O.] [BENDING]: This. Now.

(He kisses each of her eyelids.)

HELEN [V.O.]: So tender.

JOHN [V.O.]: Yes.

HELEN [V.O.]: The eyes are not mine, you know.

JOHN [V.O.]: I know.

(He kneels back, with her hand.)

Oh, it's—a virtue I miss.

HELEN [V.O.]: What?

JOHN [V.O.]: Tenderness. In me.

(He kisses her palm, speaks into it as her other hand explores in his shirt.)

HELEN: Your heart, is pounding.

JOHN [CUPS HER BREAST]: So is yours.

HELEN: Ohhh.

JOHN: Tenderness and lust is a deadly combination.

(His hand goes down her; she tenses.)

HELEN: Don't—

(He withdraws it.)

Do.

(Pause.)

JOHN [V.O.]: Jumping off a cliff is not usually considered a stable situation.

HELEN: Why, not?

JOHN [V.O.]: Teacher is why not.

HELEN: Don't, stop. Please!

(JOHN kneels up. From offstage comes the sound of ANNIE entering and he scrambles up, to head behind the platform.)

ANNIE [OFF]: Why is it so dark?

JOHN: Only for me. We have a little fire—

HELEN: Teacher says the one, experience she hasn't given me is, jail. She's wrong.

(ANNIE *onstage, in her coat, stops;* JOHN *is quick returning to* HELEN'S *hand.*)

ANNIE [STARING]: What?

JOHN [V.O.]: Our lady is here.

PETE [IN WITH PARCELS]: Where do you want these?

JOHN: Pete?

PETE: It's me, I'm sorry.

ANNIE: He was on the train—

JOHN: Well. Come in, we have a fire. Hungry?

ANNIE: No.

JOHN: How about some chili?—very tempting, I cooked, Helen washed up—

PETE: I ate.

JOHN: —made a little fire—

PETE: With our great white editor, he sacked me.

JOHN: No.

PETE: Over dessert. A gentleman, Boston cream pie.

JOHN: Oh, handsome.

PETE: I had to talk—

JOHN [TO ANNIE]: Let me have your coat. I judge a postprandial nip is called for—Irish? rock-and-rye?—

ANNIE: Brandy.

JOHN: Talk.

(*He goes behind the platform with* PETE; ANNIE *comes to* HELEN, *kneels with a bag.*)

HELEN: We made a, fire.

ANNIE [V.O.]: So I'm told. In jail?

HELEN: What?

ANNIE [V.O.]: What did I interrupt?

HELEN: Nothing.

ANNIE [V.O.]: Why jail?

HELEN: I am not, happy.

ANNIE [V.O.]: Who is? Life, liberty, and the *pursuit* of happiness; only the pursuit. Here.

HELEN: What, is it?

ANNIE [V.O.]: The journal, with your article.

HELEN: Oh.

ANNIE [V.O.]: And author's picture, very pretty. Here. The editor's check, gorgeous. Here.

HELEN: What's, this?

ANNIE [V.O.]: Something you liked on Ida.

(It's a tissue-wrapped vial of perfume, which HELEN *opens and sniffs; when* ANNIE *lights a lamp, she sees* HELEN *is crying.* ANNIE *stares.* JOHN *comes back in with two snifters of brandy,* PETE *following with another.)*

PETE: —and I don't know what he wants, a wing collar in every paragraph?

JOHN: Respect for your elders.

*(*HELEN *blunders out to the steps.)*

ANNIE: What's that about?

JOHN: The boy is a bit too pushy for that temple of—

ANNIE [CURT]: Helen. Why is she in tears?

JOHN: Oh. God knows. Listen, I have news on my book, I've placed three chapters with the *Atlantic*—

(But ANNIE *is past him to where* HELEN *huddles crying; she sits with her.)*

ANNIE [V.O.]: What is it?

HELEN [WEEPING]: I'm a, terrible person—

ANNIE [V.O.]: What happened?

(HELEN *shakes her head.* ANNIE *twists back to* JOHN.)

What happened?

JOHN: Nothing. We—

ANNIE: You made a little fire.

JOHN: Yes.

ANNIE: Which brought her to tears.

JOHN: Hey, slow down.

ANNIE: Why is she in tears?

JOHN: *I'm* not in tears, ask her.

ANNIE [V.O.]: What happened, baby?

HELEN [WEEPING]: Ask, John.

(ANNIE *stares, drops* HELEN'S *hand, and gets up.)*

ANNIE: I don't have to. Oh, you—shameless—

JOHN: Easy—

ANNIE: —cockatoo, you made love to her!

JOHN: —we have company.

ANNIE: Stop smiling!—a conquest like this? Baby, baby—

(She sits, grips HELEN'S *hand.)*

PETE [STARING]: I—can't believe—

HELEN: You know?

ANNIE [V.O.]: John made love to you.

HELEN: I, made love to, John.

ANNIE [PAUSE]: What?

PETE: I *don't* believe this!

HELEN: I'm, so ashamed.

(ANNIE *detaches herself, stands.*)

God gave me a, body and I, can't prevent what it feels. That's the, jail.

ANNIE: Oh, God help us.

HELEN: Will you, ever, forgive me?

PETE: You and Helen?—how long has this—

JOHN: Oh, shut up.

(*Offers* ANNIE *the snifter.*)

Here, steady your nerves. We kissed a bit, that's all.

ANNIE: That's all?

JOHN: That's all.

(ANNIE *swings at his face; he ducks, spilling brandy.*)

Whoa, watch it, this is life-giving stuff—

ANNIE [SAVAGE]: And next time?

(*She catches at* HELEN'S *hand, jabs into it, V.O.*)

You want John?

HELEN: Not, now—

ANNIE: You want Helen?

JOHN: Look, God gave us all bodies; it's a bit puritanical—

ANNIE: Answer yes or no!—you want her?

JOHN: Yes and no.

ANNIE: Take her.

(She pushes HELEN up at him, and marches upstairs into her dark bedroom.)

HELEN: What, what—

JOHN: Annie!

(PETE seizes HELEN'S wrist; she is shocked.)

HELEN: *You*, are here?

PETE [V.O.]: No. Goodbye.

(He drops her hand, turns—)

You're a bastard.

(—sloshes his drink at JOHN'S face, and walks out by the kitchen. JOHN gives a snifter to HELEN.)

JOHN: Cheers.

(Spells V.O.)

We're in disfavor.

(Outside PETE half turns back, is irresolute, leaves slowly.)

HELEN: How can you, joke—

(But JOHN is up the steps as ANNIE with a fistful of things— nightgown, toothbrush—comes down.)

JOHN: I'm sorry.

HELEN: —about the, pain we are, creating?

(ANNIE eludes JOHN'S hand, takes the snifter from HELEN'S en route to the desk.)

ANNIE: First of all, she doesn't drink.

HELEN [TURNS]: Teacher?

(ANNIE *thrusts her things into the empty bag;* JOHN *comes down.*)

JOHN: Look, I said I'm sorry—

ANNIE: Secondly, you can give your charge a message from me.

JOHN: *My* charge?

ANNIE: You want a few choice bits of her anatomy?—oh no, take the whole life—

HELEN: Where, are you?

ANNIE: Tell her that as of this evening—

JOHN: What are you blathering about?

ANNIE: Spell!—since I don't want to touch her, you do—tell her she's yours, twenty-four hours a day; the jailer is flying the coop.

JOHN: Oh, for God's sake. Where do you think you're going?

ANNIE: China, where's my coat?

HELEN [DESPERATE]: What is, being said?

ANNIE: Tell her.

JOHN [V.O.]: Says she's leaving.

ANNIE: I'll be at Ida and Ed's tonight; the house is yours—

JOHN: Now stop this!—you're being utterly irresponsible—

HELEN [RIGID]: Teacher.

ANNIE: Irresponsible!—oh, mother of God—

HELEN: Is she, here?

JOHN [V.O.]: Yes.

ANNIE: —give me patience with—Where's my coat!

JOHN: In the pantry!

(ANNIE *goes behind the platform;* HELEN *gropes for her.*)

HELEN: Teacher. Teacher—

JOHN [V.O.]: She isn't here.

(*—and* HELEN *throws his hand off, crying out in an inhuman guttural voice as she blunders about, collides with the couch, veers off.*)

HELEN: Teacher, Teacher, Teacher, Teacher—

(ANNIE *in her coat looks in at* HELEN.)

JOHN: What the hell am I to do with this?

ANNIE: Cope:

(*She leaves—while* HELEN *blunders about wailing—and reappears outside at the terrace table with* JOHN *running after her; he catches her arm.*)

JOHN: Dammit, you can't leave this house!

ANNIE: One of us has to; will you?

JOHN: Me? I swear—

ANNIE: Or do we throw Helen out?

JOHN: —you're a total lunatic! Now listen, what *is* serious here is—

ANNIE: Get your hands off—

JOHN: —something's dying in this house and it's me!

(HELEN *collides with the lamp on the desk, it crashes under her hands, and the desk blazes up; she screams.*)

(JOHN *runs back in,* ANNIE *after him.*)

(JOHN, *with a pillow from the couch, smothers the blaze, the room darkens as* ANNIE *swings* HELEN *away from the desk; they stumble to their knees in the fireplace glow;* ANNIE *holds her.*)

JOHN: Is she burned?

ANNIE [V.O.]: Are you burned?

HELEN: No.

JOHN: I said put electric in here a year ago.

ANNIE: We will, we will.

JOHN: When, in a cellar full of ashes?

ANNIE [V.O.]: Let me see—

HELEN: I'm fine.

ANNIE [V.O.]: You're not fine, you're a willful, tantrum-throwing, hideous brat.

HELEN: Well, why didn't you, listen to reason?

(ANNIE *lets her go, gets up.*)

If you, leave I will, smother John in his, sleep.

JOHN: *Two* lunatics.

(ANNIE *eyes him; then takes off her coat.*)

Thank you.

ANNIE: Where's my brandy?

JOHN: On the—inside the pillow, I'll get you another—

ANNIE [GOING]: I'll get it myself.

HELEN [RISES]: Are you, staying?

JOHN [V.O.]: She's staying.

HELEN: This, will not occur, again.

JOHN [V.O.]: It will be a happy memory.

HELEN: Not, happy in, structive. We must, discuss the meaning of, this event and, learn. I am not, faultless—

(ANNIE *returns with the bottle and tumbler.*)

ANNIE [OVERLAPPING]: Say I've had enough of her, go to bed.

HELEN: —but could it have, happened if John were not—

JOHN [V.O.]: She says go to bed.

HELEN: Un, forgiven?

JOHN [V.O.]: She forgives you.

ANNIE: Do I.

HELEN: Teacher?

(She reaches out a hand. ANNIE presently extends hers, to be touched; HELEN kisses it.)

Good, night.

(She stands; stops en route to the kitchen.)

Three is, one too many in, this house.

ANNIE: News.

HELEN: We need four.

JOHN: What?

HELEN: To give you, time together. I want my, mother here.

JOHN: I don't need a mother-in-law too.

HELEN: I will write, her tomorrow.

ANNIE: Over my dead body.

(HELEN blows her nose; then gropes toward the kitchen, mournful—)

HELEN: All this, fighting makes me, hungry.

(—and out. ANNIE wipes at her eyes with a finger.)

JOHN: Kissed the girls and made them cry.

ANNIE: You haven't even the grace to be embarrassed.

JOHN: I am, very; that's when I joke.

ANNIE: It's not comic.

JOHN: It's not tragic. You should cry oftener, it's very attractive.

ANNIE: Give me a reason. Not pregnant, work fifteen hours a day, find you kissing a younger woman, and you tell me you're dying in this house, what have I to cry about?

JOHN: I'm not dying.

ANNIE: I didn't think so from *her* story.

(She drinks.)

JOHN [WATCHES]: You shouldn't drink alone.

(He reaches; she edges away.)

ANNIE: Get your own glass.

JOHN [HAND OUT]: I don't want to leave you.

ANNIE: I wonder.

JOHN: Ever.

ANNIE: Why not?

JOHN: I love you, idiot.

ANNIE: Is that love?

JOHN: What else?

ANNIE: Inertia.

JOHN: All right, I'll drink out of your shoe, dammit—

(He picks up a shoe.)

—that's a classic proof.

ANNIE: Of which?

JOHN: What's this?

ANNIE: Love me, love my foot powder.

JOHN: I'll get my own glass.

ANNIE: Here. Do you make love to others too?

JOHN: No.

ANNIE: At the office?

JOHN: No.

ANNIE: Would you tell me if you did?

JOHN: No.

ANNIE: You do.

JOHN: Yes, all day long, they line up at my desk.

ANNIE: Give me my drink.

JOHN: I don't want others; it's you I want to love. I said dying—

ANNIE: Want to?

JOHN: —because loving is the juice that keeps us alive, and I feel it —draining out of me.

(ANNIE *shuts her eyes.*)

And I'm frightened. Thirty-one is no longer a—Look at me, I want to be in focus.

ANNIE [DOES]: Go on.

JOHN: *Somewhere*—

ANNIE: Why draining?

JOHN: —I'm a cog here and in that office—

ANNIE: Why draining!

JOHN: Because I'm married to a pair of Siamese twins, every time I reach for you she's in the way!

ANNIE: You reached for her.

JOHN: I'm human. But I don't seduce helpless deaf-blind virgins—

ANNIE: She's not helpless.

JOHN: —and I wasn't going to.

ANNIE: If she's helpless, my whole life has been a waste—

JOHN: Whole life is right, give *me* some of that devotion—

ANNIE [FIERCE]: I'm trying to hold it together! I do love you, I do have her on my hands every waking hour, and I expect you to feel for me when day after day I'm yanked back and forth between the two of you.

JOHN: I do.

ANNIE: No—you feel neglected, is that what you mean by loving, I'm to spoon-feed you the way I do her? I need some looking after too—

JOHN: Can I make an appointment?

ANNIE: I have a round-the-clock duty in this house!—it was never a secret—

JOHN: I didn't marry a duty!

ANNIE: Oh yes you did!—

JOHN: Then get her mother in here!

ANNIE: —it was to see Helen with my eyes, and that's what *I* mean by loving, she's our ward, and in this house we both watch over her or I don't know what you're doing in it.

JOHN [TAKEN ABACK]: Heyy—

ANNIE: Did you or did you not promise that?

JOHN: You want me out?

ANNIE: I put my life in the hands of the one man who saw me as a woman, not a doormat to Helen, and then find him in her arms—

JOHN: Now stop it—

ANNIE: —and if that's what this marriage is for I do want you out!

JOHN: Stop *ranting!*—you know you don't—

ANNIE: I don't know it!—not tonight—

JOHN: Then why didn't you leave?

ANNIE: Because I leave her to you for one minute and she's in flames!

JOHN: Sonofabitch, I—

ANNIE: You don't look after me *or* her!

JOHN: You win, you win, satisfied?

ANNIE: You look after yourself, you darling boy—

JOHN: And who else does?—all week long that office is hell by daylight, companioning youth shrinks my brain, and what little of it's left I bring home to companion you two in a house where I don't have a wife, don't have a child—

ANNIE: Ohhh—

JOHN: —which would change everything—

ANNIE: —be careful!—

JOHN: —give us both a focus—

ANNIE: —or I'll humiliate you too, me bucko, I don't have a child, you go see a doctor!

JOHN: I'll tell you one thing, the strength you've fed Helen for twenty years I find a pain in the ass as a daily diet. You're a tough morsel to digest! And if for half an hour I turn to *that* child because she needs cuddling it's the fall of the house of Usher?

ANNIE: Because it's her—can't you get that through your skull—

JOHN: She lets me feel tender! You don't.

(ANNIE *sits rigid. And covers her face; now she really cries, is wracked by it.* JOHN, *after a time, touches her.*)

JOHN [CONTINUED]: Hey—

(*She rolls away from him, and flees upstairs.*)

(JOHN *stands, walks about, drinks.* HELEN *gropes in from the kitchen with a bowl of chili.* JOHN *eyes her morosely*—)

JOHN: If I ate like you I'd be a horse.

(—and goes upstairs after ANNIE, *where he finds the bedroom empty;* PETE *returning at back looks in on* HELEN *making her way to the terrace table.)*

Bridget!

(She is, presumably, in the bathroom. JOHN *lights a cigarette, and sits on the bed with it, unhappy.)*

(Downstairs PETE *joins* HELEN *at the terrace table, sits, takes her hand.)*

HELEN: Oh. You're back.

PETE [V.O.]: Bleeding.

HELEN: I do, regret—Oh, *everything!* I'm not—good—

PETE [V.O.]: This house isn't good *for* you.

HELEN: They, love me.

PETE [V.O.]: No one in it loves only you.

HELEN: And who, could?

PETE [V.O.]: Someone. Who is free to.

(Long pause.)

HELEN: Free. Is not a word I—ever knew—

PETE: Teacher won't be with you always. I can.

HELEN: I'm—frightened—

(They go in, PETE *with his arm around* HELEN.)

(Upstairs, ANNIE *comes dolefully into the bedroom towelling her face; looks at* JOHN.)

ANNIE: I didn't say I was lovable, you did.

JOHN: Are you all right?

ANNIE: Radiant, I just threw up.

JOHN: Oh, God. I say things, half of it's literature—

(ANNIE *discards the towel. She starts to undress; sits opposite him on the bed.*)

ANNIE: You do want to leave me.

JOHN: I didn't say *that.*

ANNIE: I have ears.

JOHN: Then let's listen. That bit of dalliance I drifted into down-stairs was—like the bell that rings in the bay, headed for the rocks, change course. Can't we?

ANNIE: Change *how?*—become a shrinking violet—?

JOHN: You change, I'll change.

ANNIE: Is there time?

JOHN: Oh God, yes.

ANNIE: Then I have this thought. If Ida and Ed can manage it, do —something of what I do with—Oh, my heart is not easy—

JOHN: What?

ANNIE: Helen. They offered.

JOHN: Offered what?

ANNIE: To put her up. I can't live like this!

JOHN: What are we talking about?

ANNIE: I want to go away with you.

JOHN [AMAZED]: Leave Helen?

ANNIE: Maybe a winter cruise?

JOHN: Leave Helen—that *is* a change—

ANNIE: Lie on a beach and—Oh Johnny, tears?

JOHN: No, I'm a big boy, I—Yes. I'm honored, I—

ANNIE: Come here.

JOHN: —never thought I'd hear that—

ANNIE [HUGS HIM]: Why is it with Helen the minute trouble rears its head I see the solution, like that! And with others—you—I'm so blind to—

(JOHN *stops her mouth with his*—)

JOHN: She inspires you. Mortals don't.

(—*and kisses her throat; his hand caresses her body, thigh, groin.*)

ANNIE: You're doing well enough. Love me. Love me.

JOHN: Oh, I'll think about it.

ANNIE: As I am—

JOHN: I'll think about it.

(*He begins to unbutton her skirt, between kisses.*)

ANNIE: Will you love me as I am if I change enough?

Lights Fade.

ACT THREE

ACT III

Daylight rises in the empty house. In the interval the mail has accumulated—on the floor a U.S. mail sack, on the couch some parcels. A moment passes while music dies away.

THEN HELEN, IN WINTER COAT, BLUNDERS IN FROM THE KITCHEN AS FAST AS SHE CAN; SHE BUMPS INTO THE CHAIR. AT THE COUCH SHE SITS DOWN ON A PARCEL, JUMPS UP, FLINGS IT ANYWHERE, AND THROWS HERSELF PRONE.

PETE HURRIES IN FROM THE KITCHEN, AND STANDS, WATCHING HER.

PETE: Oh, Jesus.

(He comes to kneel beside her; hesitates; then takes her hand to spell.)

Helen, dear—

(She yanks it away, averts. He gets up, goes to the front entrance, looks off; comes back, squats to take her hand from the other side, spelling.)

They're coming now.

HELEN: Already?

(She sits up.)

I look, terrible—

PETE [V.O.]: Must you be here?

HELEN [WITH DIGNITY]: I don't, have many, choices.

PETE [V.O.]: Can't we wait? I'd rather wait to—

HELEN: I want, Teacher.

PETE [V.O.]: What will we tell her?

HELEN: The, truth.

PETE [V.O.]: I don't want to see them.

HELEN: Then, go.

PETE [V.O.]: Helen, you can blame everything on me—

HELEN: I do!

PETE [V.O.]: I feel—ghastly, about—

(Voices audible offstage, approaching; PETE *backs away—)*

ANNIE [OFF]: I said inexcusable.

ED [OFF]: I had no idea what was going on—

ANNIE [OFF]: You could have written!

JOHN [OFF]: Where, to the Sargasso Sea?

ANNIE [ON]: Cable!—the ship! Marconi is unheard of in Boston?

(—and they are outside, in topcoats, lugging suitcases; PETE *retreats half up the stairs out of their view.)*

We were not on a raft.

ED: It all happened three days ago!

ANNIE: I am to be informed of what happens to Helen when it happens!

(Inside, she stops, seeing HELEN. *And sits to take her hand;* HELEN *throws her arms around her; they hold, in a long hug.* ED *and* JOHN *set down the suitcases at the steps.)*

ED: And I couldn't get anything out of either of them.

ANNIE [OVER HELEN'S SHOULDER]: You left her alone here?

ED: I left her at home!—with Ida, I don't know what she's doing here—

ANNIE [NOT SPELLING]: Let me see you.

HELEN: Hold, me.

JOHN [WATCHING]: Thought that was Pete's job now.

(He clears the parcels from the couch; HELEN *hugs* ANNIE.)

HELEN: Oh, I missed you!

JOHN: How did you find out?

ED: Ida read it in the *Globe*.

ANNIE: The newspapers?

ED: Well, Pete filed the marriage license.

ANNIE: What a field day for the garbage rats!

ED: They were all out here. Why that young idiot thought Helen Keller could sign a marriage license and no one notice eludes me.

ANNIE: Where is he?

ED [EXASPERATED]: I don't know!

JOHN: Probably after Ida, he's an enterprising boy. I need a drink. Anybody?

(He picks up the floor parcel, and ED *walks with him toward the kitchen;* ANNIE *touches* HELEN'S *face.)*

ED: How were things at sea?

JOHN: Finished the first draft. Up at dawn—

ED: I meant Teacher.

JOHN: Had a marvellous time.

(He goes off; ED *turns back.)*

ANNIE [V.O.]: I have one question. Are you happy?

HELEN: De, lirious.

ED: I don't like your color.

ANNIE [STARING AT HELEN]: What color would you like?—I was green the first week—

ED: Any bleeding?

ANNIE: Yes.

ED: Well, you can't keep leaking blood.

ANNIE: I can't talk about it now.

(Spells V.O.)

What's wrong?

HELEN: Who, is here?

ANNIE [V.O.]: Doctor Ed. John.

HELEN: I'll, wait.

ANNIE [V.O.]: Where is Pete?

HELEN: He, ran away.

ED: What!

ANNIE [NOT SPELLING]: Ran away—

ED: Sonofabitch!—excuse it, now he's let *all* of us down—

(PETE *descends as* JOHN *comes in with a drink.)*

JOHN: Well, there's the lucky fellow!—

PETE: I didn't run away—

JOHN: —you've kicked up a lot of dust here.

PETE: —and I'm not a young idiot, thank you.

ED: Idiot is kind!—I'd like to break your damn neck—

JOHN: Gently, doctor.

PETE: I did nothing to apologize to *you* for.

ED: Abuse my hospitality?—I was responsible for her!—

ANNIE [ON HER FEET]: Stop.

ED: —every day in my house helping Ida with this innocent, how the hell did I know what he was after?

JOHN: Didn't Ida?

ED: Ida's an idiot too!

ANNIE: This is pointless. Pete, sit down.

JOHN: How do you plan to support her?

PETE [IN THE CHAIR]: I don't, now. What we—

JOHN: You're not moving in here, buster.

ANNIE: That's not the issue. Pete, I have one question.

PETE: Why would I move in here?

(ED *sits to pat* HELEN'S *hand.*)

I did think I'd be—her right hand, serve, I wanted to really serve, because—

ANNIE: You are an idiot.

PETE: —because she deserves better.

ANNIE: Thank you, who doesn't?

PETE: You have your lives, you go away and—

HELEN [TO ED]: I've made a, mess.

ANNIE: I must know one thing.

PETE: None of this is Helen's fault.

ANNIE: Good. Do you love her?

PETE: Well—

ANNIE: *Well!*

PETE: I—yes, well, it's complicated, because it—changed, after all the newspapers, those reporters at the windows, like a fishbowl, everything was—oh, it's so embarrassing—

ANNIE: And that's the *rock* of this marriage?

PETE: What?

ANNIE: Embarrassment?

PETE: We didn't get married.

(ANNIE *darts a glance at* HELEN; ED *is on his feet spluttering.*)

ED: You—what—

JOHN: You said they did, Ed, you got all my hopes up.

ED: I believe the newspapers!

PETE: We didn't use the license.

ANNIE: She did sign a marriage license?

PETE: Yes.

(ANNIE *moves to* HELEN, *kneels spelling.*)

ANNIE [V.O.]: Are you in trouble?

HELEN: I want to, talk alone.

ANNIE [V.O.]: Are you pregnant!

HELEN: Of course, not. From, what?

ANNIE [V.O.] [FLAT]: Do you love him?

HELEN: Oh, he is so, *boring*.

(*A silence.* JOHN *then puts his hand on* PETE—)

JOHN: Pete, old boy.

(—*who after a moment covers his blinking eyes with a hand.*)

ANNIE: I didn't tell her you were here—

PETE: Don't.

(*He gets up*—)

Don't—tell her—

(—and walks out by the kitchen; outside rear, he is visible on the run.)

ED: I was hard on the boy—

JOHN: I'll start cheering him up tomorrow. Hell, he's better off out of it, he knows that, got in over his head—

ANNIE [v.o.]: Then why?

HELEN: Why, what?

ANNIE [v.o.]: This farce!

HELEN: Send them, away.

ANNIE [RISES]: I want to talk to her—

JOHN: Here.

(He gives her the drink.)

ED: I want to talk to you.

ANNIE: I can't now—I have a biting headache—

JOHN: Needs a winter cruise. Oh, the peace of—

ANNIE: One's enough, it did this.

JOHN: Did what?—it *is* a farce—

ANNIE: And one step from a disaster. She needed me.

JOHN: I swear, you're like a lover, off the boat and into her heart.

ANNIE: And I wasn't here.

JOHN: You were with your husband! Did I hallucinate what took place on that voyage?

ANNIE: I can't feel blameless—

JOHN: Work, love, it's all I ever wanted, the minute we step over that threshold it unravels.

ANNIE: —and it frightens me.

JOHN: And reneging on everything you said doesn't?

(He walks out into the kitchen.)

ANNIE: Now he's biting—

ED: I want you to make a decision.

ANNIE: I can't *think* about that now!—my head is splitting—

ED: Don't drink then, it dilates the capillaries.

(ANNIE *swallows a gulp.*)

You're the worst kind of patient, a know-it-all mule. I'll talk to your husband.

(He goes after JOHN. ANNIE *settles next to* HELEN.)

ANNIE [V.O.]: What happened?

HELEN: Are we, alone?

ANNIE [V.O.]: Yes.

HELEN: He, lied.

ANNIE [V.O.]: To all of us.

HELEN: To himself. It was all a, delirium. Of one foolish dream wrapped in, another so—noble; I wanted to free you—

ANNIE [NOT SPELLING]: Oh, Helen.

HELEN: And be, free. Not noble.

ANNIE [V.O.]: Without love?

HELEN: He *said* he, loved me.

ANNIE [NOT SPELLING]: Ohhh—

HELEN: I was over, joyed. And we would share, my work and life—

ANNIE [V.O.]: Words.

HELEN: Yes. I never thought, and when he sees your eyes in a, saucer? He was, in my room, that day.

ANNIE [v.o.]: When?

HELEN: After the, license.

ANNIE [v.o.]: And?

HELEN: He couldn't, make love to me.

(Pause.)

ANNIE [v.o.]: Baby. Sometimes that—

HELEN: Don't call me, baby. You have always, made me feel, normal.

ANNIE [v.o.]: Yes.

HELEN: I'm a, freak. I'm a, freak!

(ANNIE *clasps her hand tight.* ED *walks off, outside;* JOHN *comes in, stands.)*

So. My problem is to, *live,* in this world. How, and where, now?

ANNIE [v.o.]: Here, here.

HELEN: It's not, my house.

JOHN: Of course it is.

(He sits in a chair near them; he is very quiet.)

Why didn't you tell me?

ANNIE [SHE KNOWS]: What?

JOHN: The hysterectomy.

ANNIE: I thought I must—wait. Wait until—

JOHN: No. He says not, I say not.

HELEN: Is, John here?

ANNIE [v.o.]: Yes.

HELEN [RISES]: I'll go, upstairs.

(JOHN takes her hand as she passes.)

JOHN [V.O.]: Stay.

ANNIE: It means I can't give you a child.

JOHN: I've managed thirty years without.

(He brings HELEN'S *hand to his lips, speaks across it to* ANNIE.)

He sees no evidence of myosarcoma, now. If you're worried. It *is* a question of losing blood.

HELEN: Who?

JOHN: Teacher.

(HELEN *starts.)*

Don't be alarmed. It does mean a hospital stay; she'll need both of us.

HELEN: What is, it?

ANNIE: I'll tell her.

(She rises.)

Get out of these—glad rags—

(She takes HELEN'S *arm; at the steps when she bends for her suitcase,* HELEN *gropes for it.)*

Oh, no—

HELEN: Please.

JOHN: Let her.

(So ANNIE *lets her.* HELEN *lugs it upstairs, off;* JOHN *sits pondering.* ANNIE *starts up.)*

Listen.

(He is facing out; she stops.)

I feel stupid. My complaints are picayune. This last month with you was the happiest of my life. I need you. Alive and well, and there's nothing I won't do to keep you kicking.

(A pause.)

ANNIE: I love you, Johnny.

JOHN: I love you too.

(She goes up.)

(JOHN *after a moment gets up, takes the mail sack, hefts it—)*

Ah, fame.

(—and carries it to the kitchen, as lights fade.)

(Music, time passing—weeks—)

(into twilight, the room empty. HELEN *comes down the steps; she has a tumbler and a pill. She waits at the couch, offering them.)*

HELEN: Here.

(Presently she gropes on the couch.)

Teacher?

(She makes for the kitchen.)

Teacher!

(ANNIE, *in nightwrap and shawl, coming in with a mug, pats* HELEN'S *outstretched hand.)*

You, get back on, that couch.

ANNIE [V.O.]: My behind hurts.

HELEN: Doctor Ed said, complete rest.

ANNIE [V.O.]: Rest is ruining me.

(But she goes—walking carefully, in some discomfort—)

HELEN: Take, your pill.

(—and ANNIE *stops to take her pill, drinking from her own mug; lies back on the couch on a pillow.)*

How are your, insides?

ANNIE [MUTTERING]: Doing well. Somewhere. One future the less.

HELEN [HAND OUT]: Are you in, pain?

ANNIE [V.O.] [TAKES IT]: Not from the knife.

HELEN: I'll get the, checkers.

ANNIE [V.O.] [STOPS HER]: Don't pause after an article.

HELEN: What?

ANNIE [V.O.]: It's not how we speak.

HELEN: Why?

ANNIE [V.O.]: Pause after nouns and verbs, if you must, not after articles or prepositions.

HELEN: Pause. After nouns. And verbs. Satis, fied?

ANNIE [V.O.]: Dissatisfied. Useless, bored, don't humor me. I intend to work every day now on your voice.

HELEN: What for?

ANNIE [V.O.]: Clarity. And strength.

HELEN: To what, end?

ANNIE [V.O.]: We can't live on writing. We'll get a singing teacher for you.

HELEN: We can't, live on, singing!

ANNIE [V.O.]: Wrong.

HELEN: We, can?

ANNIE [V.O.]: Think.

HELEN: Oh. We can't live. On singing.

ANNIE [V.O.]: I'm pondering a different future—

(JOHN, *in topcoat and hat, hurries in, front, with two grocery bags and briefcase.*)

JOHN: Ladies, ladies, good evening—sorry I'm late, I missed the four-ten—missed you—

ANNIE: Missed you.

(JOHN *kisses her, puts a bag in* HELEN'S *hands—*)

JOHN: I was in Lawrence. Big strike—

(—*and takes his briefcase to the steps;* HELEN *has her nose in the bag.*)

HELEN: Ahhh—

JOHN: Mocha Java. Steak tonight—

ANNIE: Ida cooked a pot roast.

JOHN: —pot roast tomorrow. Lawrence is boiling. The mills are out, the Wobblies are in, streets jammed, militia, anarchists, it's like the French Revolution—

(*He recaptures the bag from* HELEN, *takes both bags into the kitchen, hollering from there.*)

—if the Wobblies can organize textiles from top to bottom there's no end in sight—

ANNIE [V.O.] [MEANWHILE]: May I get up?

HELEN: No.

JOHN [BACK IN]: —and even the children are marching; I came back planning a piece for *Youth's Companion*, those damn *dotards!* Macy the monster, they skinned me alive—

(*Spells to* HELEN *V.O.*)

Shall I make us a fire?

HELEN: After, supper.

JOHN [SMACKS HIS HANDS]: A fire!—and tonight we finish *Paradise Lost*—

ANNIE [UNDER HER BREATH]: Thank God.

JOHN: —it ends beautifully—

ANNIE: It ends?

JOHN: What?

ANNIE: Stop bubbling over.

JOHN [A PAUSE]: Am I?

(He turns to the desk, pours a drink.)

ANNIE: Sit. You haven't written in weeks.

JOHN: I write all day long.

ANNIE: On the book.

JOHN: Well.

ANNIE: I want you to finish.

JOHN: I can't work up much interest in Henry James when—

ANNIE: Spell. Please.

(JOHN takes the chair, spelling to HELEN on the floor between them.)

I've learned one thing this winter, I feed on my work with Helen. You must be starved for yours.

JOHN: It's a pleasure to be needed. No?

HELEN: Yes.

ANNIE: I've taken up the whole winter—

(She stifles the spelling—)

—and you're drinking too much.

(—*and unstifles it.*)

I'd like you to quit.

JOHN: Liquor's a relaxation I permit—

ANNIE: The magazine.

JOHN: Quit the magazine.

ANNIE: And finish the book.

JOHN [SPELLING THROUGHOUT]: And live on what?—it pays half the bills in this shack—

ANNIE: I have a way. With Helen.

HELEN: What, way?

ANNIE: Lecture.

HELEN [PAUSE, INCREDULOUS]: Lec, ture?

ANNIE: For the women's clubs.

JOHN: Hey.

ANNIE: There's a living in it. For all three of us.

JOHN [THINKING]: Could be—

ANNIE: It means continual work with Helen—cure me much faster than this couch—and you write. Full time.

HELEN: Lecture. On what, topic?

ANNIE: Life.

HELEN: On the, moon?

ANNIE: John will tell us.

JOHN: Well. You tell your story, of course. It's not a crazy idea—

HELEN: The, needs of the, blind!

ANNIE: We'll go out and wake the world up.

HELEN: It sounds im, possible. Let's!

(ANNIE *passes her mug;* HELEN *drinks.*)

ANNIE: May we?

JOHN: Hell, I'll draft it.

HELEN: There's, rum in it.

ANNIE [V.O.]: To celebrate.

HELEN: Two, lady lecturers, getting potted!

ANNIE [V.O.]: May I get up?

(HELEN *pulls her to her feet.*)

HELEN: Cook. John is, awful.

(To JOHN.*)*

Teasing.

(She makes for the kitchen. JOHN *still sits.* ANNIE *after a step turns back.*)

ANNIE: Johnny.

JOHN: Yes?

ANNIE: Are you getting tired of the struggle?

JOHN [PAUSE]: What struggle?—it's life.

ANNIE: Are you getting tired?

JOHN: No.

(But, as she leaves, he drinks.)

(Music—much time passing—until dusk comes up on the terrace table, where ED *sits alone with a tumbler of whiskey; another tumbler and bottle empty.)*

ED: Just tell him. Stop. And that's my last word. Where the hell is he?

(JOHN comes out, opening a bottle; he is in an apron, and both are much in their cups.)

JOHN: Reinforcements.

(He sits, pours into both tumblers.)

ED: Stop. And that's my last word.

JOHN: Stop what?

ED: Drinking. Pour it on Helen's roses, before meals.

JOHN: You're no gardener, it'll kill them.

ED: Exactly.

JOHN: To the ladies.

(They drink.)

ED: Any news there?

JOHN: Due back tomorrow. Between lectures. Helen writes they're—

(He digs a letter out of his pocket, unfolds it.)

—having a triumph; in Canada everyone—Here, "everyone said we were wonderful, fascinating, charming and beautiful women."

ED: Everyone is right.

JOHN: And good providers, a check for the groceries. Well, they're raking the money in. "I am now—"

ED: I liked your book.

JOHN: Past history.

ED: Damn good reading on American literature. Can't read the literature.

JOHN: I didn't write that book for you and me.

ED: Oh?

JOHN: Wrote it for my children.

(This hangs; both thinking.)

ED: Wasn't any choice, Johnny.

JOHN: Well. "I am now a member of the Los Angeles local of the Socialist Party."

ED: Helen? I'll be damned.

JOHN: So I'm not without some influence on the future. Workers, unite!—something big is coming. Don't know why I'm here, keeping the pots company on the back burner—

ED: This damn rotgut—

(He drains his tumbler.)

Came over to bring you to dinner, Ida has a big sirloin.

JOHN [BACK TO THE LETTER]: I like a woman with a big sirloin, watch out.

ED: Don't tell her I'm drunk.

(He starts out, unsteady.)

JOHN: I admire my lady's achievements, you know.

(But when he looks up, ED is gone. Then JOHN, alone, grimly crushes the letter in his fist.)

From the back burner—

(Lights down on him, up to full daylight in the house; and from the landing HELEN and ANNIE descend, HELEN in fancy dress, their voices attempting a scale—they stop for HELEN to feel ANNIE'S throat, ANNIE sings on key, HELEN then singing wildly off key. They pass so behind the platform, an inhuman duet.)

(Lights to full again on JOHN, without apron, reading a newspaper at the terrace table. The singing makes him wince.)

JOHN: Shades of Schubert.

(HELEN'S *vocalizing continues offstage as* ANNIE *comes out with a breakfast tray, with letters; she wears dark glasses.*)

ANNIE: May I join you?

JOHN: Delighted.

ANNIE: Need anything?

JOHN: Everyone who isn't on a picket line is in jail. Maybe I should try jail.

ANNIE: I *won't* join you.

JOHN: Some great books were written in jail—

ANNIE [GIVES IT]: There's a letter for you. And that's the check from Helen, for the strikers. With a message.

JOHN [SCANS THE MESSAGE]: Yes, she's a good comrade.

ANNIE: I find her so. Lifts my spirits—

JOHN [THE CHECK]: And benefactor.

ANNIE: And with audiences it's extraordinary, you *feel* the hope coming up in them, like a tide—

JOHN: Ahuh.

ANNIE: —of joy in her, they laugh, cry, it's unbelievable what a gift she has for—

JOHN: Yes, you told me.

ANNIE: I'm boring you.

JOHN: Is Italy possible this year?

ANNIE: Italy?

JOHN: I'd get some writing done, shed a tear at Keats's grave—

ANNIE: We can't; we're tied down with these—

JOHN: By myself. Five hundred dollars would give me the summer.

ANNIE: I haven't seen you all winter.

JOHN: I was here.

ANNIE: It was also lonesome out there.

JOHN: Here too, but such is life.

ANNIE: We're—like strangers.

JOHN: Not fighting.

ANNIE: Is that enough? We don't—talk—

JOHN: Well, I'm something of a stranger to myself. Living in the shadow of such celebrity, things get lost, like who's who.

(He lifts his drink.)

I need some sunlight, sweet.

ANNIE: And I'm not it.

JOHN: You have Helen, I have Italy and a new book in mind.

ANNIE: What about?

JOHN: Socialism in America.

ANNIE: On her capital?

JOHN: That's illiterate.

ANNIE: No. Since Helen's making money—

JOHN: Private life and class forces are not synonymous.

ANNIE: I can't shake off the feeling you think she's a kind of sponge. Squeeze and drink.

JOHN [STARES]: Dammit, that's bitchy.

ANNIE: It's not very wholesome for any of us; I—

JOHN [GETS UP]: Who talked me into this largesse?

ANNIE: —don't like the thought she's being used. It was to finish a book. Not to start—

JOHN: I don't like it either!

ANNIE: —a way of life in which you ask less and less of yourself.

JOHN: You call every tune without me, pay the piper!

(He catches up the glass, check, message, bottle.)

When you're gone I long for you; come back and I—

(Stops, jerks his head at HELEN'S *vocalizing.)*

—can't stand our song. Next engagement the Met?

ANNIE: Is that your hope?

JOHN: Terror; I believe you could do it.

ANNIE: It strengthens her voice, to lecture.

*(*JOHN *is on his way in—)*

For *money.*

(—and he stops.)

JOHN: Oh, you're a comrade.

(He goes in behind the platform. ANNIE *sits over her tray, disgusted with herself.)*

ANNIE: Mouthful of boils.

*(*HELEN'S *singing ceases;* JOHN *comes waltzing her into the office, laughing.)*

JOHN: Here we go round the mulberry bush, the mulberry bush, the mulberry bush, so early in the morning and look at her—

(Spells V.O. Outside, ANNIE *rises to come in with the letter.)*

You look ravishing.

HELEN [VOICE NOTICEABLY IMPROVED]: I'm a new woman. It's my intention, to ravish a man, named Harry Weber.

JOHN [V.O.]: Today?

HELEN: At lunch.

JOHN [V.O.]: The way to a man's heart, even a vaudeville agent's.

(He sits HELEN *on the couch; she sniffs.)*

I need your help, dear Helen, a little favor. If I can borrow—

HELEN: John. You said, you would stop.

JOHN [V.O.]: I did, not ten minutes ago.

HELEN: You must, or whom can Teacher, lean on? Her eyes are, failing—

JOHN [NOT SPELLING]: Not her tongue.

HELEN: In Buffalo, she fell downstairs.

JOHN [V.O.]: What?

HELEN: She didn't tell you?

JOHN [V.O.]: No.

HELEN: I, count on you. What, favor?

JOHN [V.O.]: Forget it. Look, I know I'm a fifth wheel now—

HELEN: No.

JOHN [V.O.]: —but I'll try. I'll try, I'll try! We'll give her a rest.

*(*ANNIE *comes in.)*

HELEN: How?

JOHN [V.O.]: I've been meaning to read *Das Kapital* with you, in the German. Dip you like the baby Achilles in the source—

HELEN: Ahh.

ANNIE: You left your letter.

(She drops it on the couch, and goes to the desk; JOHN *regards the couchful.)*

JOHN: Letters, letters, letters—

HELEN: I look forward.

ANNIE: Under Marx they'll be edible; *I* look forward.

JOHN: The voice of doom is heard in the land.

(HELEN *waggles her hand;* JOHN *spells, V.O.)*

What's the greatest invention in history?

HELEN: The wheel.

JOHN [V.O.]: The wheelbarrow, it taught the Irish to walk on two legs.

HELEN [LAUGHS]: I'll use that, with Mr. Weber.

(JOHN *opens his letter.)*

John, you *can* help.

JOHN: Ha.

ANNIE: Something?

JOHN: Oh, the Rand School.

ANNIE: Who?

JOHN: In New York, they want some courses, rebellion in American literature—

ANNIE: That's fine.

JOHN [TOSSES IT ASIDE]: Five dollars a night?—

ANNIE: It's a compliment—

JOHN: —it's not the Keith-Albee circuit.

ANNIE: How many nights would it be?

JOHN: Drop it.

ANNIE: You might make it a book—

JOHN: Drop it.

HELEN: Is anyone, in this house?

(ANNIE *comes to her hand, spells the subsequent talk.)*

Thank you. John—

JOHN: What can I do for you?

HELEN: Criticize, my speech.

ANNIE [V.O.]: No.

HELEN: I want, John's opinion.

ANNIE [V.O.]: Not now.

HELEN: Now. I value it. Mr. Weber says, people come to vaudeville, for a laugh.

JOHN: You're giving him the lecture?

HELEN: He thinks, I'm lugubrious.

ANNIE [NODS]: Reduced to one-third.

JOHN: Price?

ANNIE: Length.

HELEN [PLACING HERSELF]: Say what looks, wrong. It means money. A great deal—

JOHN: How much?

ANNIE: It doesn't matter—

HELEN: —a thousand dollars a week.

(Long pause.)

JOHN: Vaudeville. I told you the Met.

HELEN [THE SPEECH]: My teacher has told you, how a word from her hand, touched the darkness of my mind. Through love, I found my soul and God and happiness.

JOHN: Don't wave, it's peculiar.

HELEN: Alone, we can do so little. Together, so much. Only love—

(ANNIE interrupts her, spells.)

Where shall I put them? In my mouth?

JOHN: No, that's for the foot. Hold a flower or something. Here—

(He is up, ducks behind the platform; ANNIE *moves—)*

ANNIE: I'll get a book.

(—and is at the desk when JOHN, *returning with the bottle, puts it in* HELEN'S *hand. She goes rigid.* ANNIE *is grim.)*

HELEN: Take this back.

ANNIE: John.

JOHN: That's funny.

ANNIE: It's not funny.

JOHN: Oh, come off it, you expect me to take this seriously?— vaudeville!

ANNIE: It's our way of reaching a public—

JOHN: You'll be out on that stage with jugglers—

ANNIE: —about the blind in this country—

JOHN: —doxies in tights, trained seals—

HELEN [SIMULTANEOUS]: What is he, saying?

*(*ANNIE *spells to her.)*

JOHN: —with *your* trained seal, mouthing platitudes. Found God and happiness, for Christ sake.

HELEN: I'm, religious.

ANNIE: Not platitudes, she has an experience to share—

JOHN: Then let her talk in church!

HELEN: I know, how shabby that stage, is—

JOHN: You're exhibiting her for money!

ANNIE: No.

HELEN: —but where I speak, doesn't matter—

JOHN: She's a socialist, stands for a world where men and women live in dignity, not go out with dog acts to do a spiritual shimmy dance while children are dying in misery, dammit, it's enough her relatives are lynching black boys, everywhere you look—

ANNIE: Oh, stop it.

JOHN: —it's a famine, her comrades are in jail for a dime more a day to keep the wolf from their throats and you're training her for vaudeville! At a thousand dollars a week. And I have to *beg*, for Italy?

HELEN: He's drunk, he doesn't mean, all he says—

JOHN: I am not—drunk!—but I do have this sober word.

(He speaks into HELEN'S *palm.)*

You've been badly advised.

HELEN: By whom?

JOHN: The iron maiden. Teacher! You're a symbol—

ANNIE: Oh, God give me patience—

JOHN: —you value my opinion?—you mustn't do what she says.

HELEN: I am earning, *our* living!

ANNIE [SPINS HIM]: Get away from her.

JOHN: Why?—I'll preempt your private kingdom?—all she ever knows is what you tell her. Go, lock her up—

*(*HELEN *turns;* ANNIE *twists her back, spelling.)*

ANNIE: Stay and hear!—what he wants is five hundred dollars to go to Italy.

HELEN: What?

JOHN: Four, and I'll take myself out of your eyes—

ANNIE: Four. Will you take three?

JOHN [GRITTY]: —get you out of mine—

HELEN: Don't, don't say things—

ANNIE: Talk to her!

HELEN: —we can't live with—

JOHN: Ho, get through her ears?—they're full of your chatter, insinuations against me—

ANNIE [NOT SPELLING]: Never. I never—

(HELEN'S *hand flies to her face, lip-reading.*)

JOHN: I'll tell you one thing is never, you've never been worth shit as a wife to me!—

ANNIE: Oh, you picked a day for this!—

JOHN: —I did better with the tarts in Scollay Square—

ANNIE: —is that what you hope, ruin today for her?

JOHN: —and it's a damned poor life I have here, starving by inches—

ANNIE [PUTS HELEN'S HAND DOWN]: Go back to your tarts!

(*She turns* HELEN *to the steps;* JOHN *spins* HELEN *back, claps her hand to his own mouth.*)

JOHN: No, hear me out. It's an offer, Helen, you—

ANNIE [PULLS]: Leave her alone!—you'll—

JOHN: Shut up for once!—you can do better—

ANNIE: —you will not upset her further just when this man is—

JOHN: —better than the hag-ridden life *you'll* have with her, turning into a tin showpiece. Leave her!—

ANNIE: What! Oh, you—

JOHN: —come! come to Italy with me!—get out—

ANNIE: —jealous!—jealous fool—

JOHN: —before she nags you to death the way she's nagged me to—

ANNIE: I nagged you into two books!—

JOHN: You're a nag, a nag, a man-eating nag I can't stand the sight of any—

ANNIE: —because you're such a boozy charmer you disgust—

HELEN [SCREAMING]: Stop it, you two!

(A silence.)

Must I, protect her from you?

(Then ANNIE *takes* HELEN'S *hand to her mouth.)*

ANNIE: Give him the five hundred, it's what he wants.

JOHN: What I want is myself back!

HELEN: John. I didn't invite, talk about money. But my earnings, have paid for your writing, and club, and tailor, and charities; and your liquor. And I expect, if you don't stop, I'll pay, for your funeral. What I earn, is for Teacher. You will not have, a penny more.

*(*JOHN *wheels, wanders with the bottle here, there;* ANNIE *puts a hand on his arm.)*

ANNIE: John. John—

JOHN: Oh, you've done it now, haven't you.

(He breaks away, in a jig-step—)

Love. John loves Teacher. Teacher loves Helen. Helen and Teacher love John, and John loves Helen and Teacher. John and Helen and Teacher are one huge love turd. Through love—

(—and bumps against the desk—)

—I found my soul and God and happiness!

(—and smashes the bottle on the typewriter. He goes to his knees and ANNIE *comes to kneel too; he is wild.)*

ANNIE: Oh, John honey, we do love you—

JOHN: You're killing me!

(He throws her off, she falls. He rounds to stalk HELEN.*)*

Not a penny, hey?—who corrected your goddam commas, you
leech, who taught you how to turn every paragraph you published, who helped in—I *shaped* this claptrap lecture!—

(He seizes her by the wrist, wrathful in her terrified face; ANNIE
comes up with the letter knife.)

—and you've sucked us empty, angel, you've gutted her life and
mine, and I swear if I could—wipe out the day you were born—

ANNIE: You hurt her I *will* kill you.

(She catches JOHN *by the arm; he falls back from the knife in her
hand. A silence.)*

JOHN [GRIM]: Yes. It's next to murder, isn't it. Love.

(ANNIE *half unbelieving throws the knife away from her. She
turns* HELEN *to sit on the couch;* HELEN *is unsteady.)*

HELEN: Teacher—

ANNIE [V.O.]: It's all right.

(But she is trembling, walks around; JOHN *picks up the knife, to
drop on the desk, and stands over it.)*

JOHN: It's not all right.

ANNIE: No. We've gone bad here. This year.

JOHN: Meaning me.

ANNIE: Both of us. Both, oh Johnny, I didn't mean the things we
said. And the money is nothing, Italy's no problem—but is that
what you want me to give you?

JOHN: No.

ANNIE: And what I want to give I can't.

JOHN: I know that.

ANNIE: It's doing us all harm now. You most.

JOHN: Yes.

ANNIE: And to make something new of yourself here, no, I think you should—be free of us—

JOHN [TURNS]: Ah?

ANNIE: It's a dead end. I'm tired of the struggle, too.

(JOHN, *after a wait, wheels upstairs, to pick up pages at his typewriter, and comes down—*)

JOHN: Good. Good. Good, good, good—I'll write you. There's a world out there cracking open, maybe it's my oyster, where's my—where's—

(*—and finds his letter, and catches up the jacket at the terrace table; stops.*)

Oh, Bridget—I thought I could do better. I didn't mean the things *I* said.

(*He crosses front and out. Now* ANNIE *falls apart; goes to her knees, cries—*)

ANNIE: Johnny!

(*—and in that position is found by* HELEN *groping.* ANNIE *rolls away in revulsion; she wheels here and there in the room, glares at* HELEN, *and flees into the kitchen; out back she ducks among branches, weeping, stumbling out of sight.*)

(*Lights begin to die, on* HELEN *alone; she gropes to the stairs.*)

(*Music, time passing.*)

(*Dusk comes up in the house.* ANNIE *is covering furniture with dustcloths; outside,* ED *comes out to the terrace table, and carries it in behind the platform. From upstairs* HELEN *in overcoat, with another in her arms, descends.)*

(ED *comes in.)*

ED: Moving day is always pensive.

ANNIE: The table goes.

ED: I'm sorry you sold the place.

ANNIE: Too many ghosts.

ED: I'll miss you good ladies.

ANNIE: And we're travellers now.

(ED *carries the table out;* ANNIE *leans at the banister, where* HELEN *touches her.)*

(ED *re-enters, to the couch.)*

ED: This stays?

ANNIE: On the porch. Lighthouse wants it.

(Together they lift it, take it to the terrace.)

ED: I saw Johnny in New York. Working there.

ANNIE: Oh. Did he look well?

ED: Drinking like a fish. But expecting.

ANNIE: Expecting what?

(ED *stops.)*

ED: Shouldn't have said that.

ANNIE [STRICKEN]: A baby?

ED: Yes.

ANNIE [PAUSE]: Who is she?

ED: I shouldn't have—

ANNIE: Who is she?

ED: A sculptress.

ANNIE: Young?

ED: I believe so.

ANNIE: Pretty?

ED: I didn't meet her.

ANNIE [PAUSE]: A quiet type, I hope.

ED: She's a deaf-mute.

(ANNIE *is moveless; and after a moment* ED *leaves.*)

HELEN: Teacher. And once again, Teacher—

(ANNIE *turns to stare.*)

It will be my answer, in the dark. When death, calls.

(*A silence.*)

It's a poem.

(*And presently* ANNIE *comes back, takes her hand.*)

ANNIE [V.O.]: I am not—seeing well—

HELEN: I will be, your eyes.

ANNIE [V.O.] [SMILES]: Not yet; give the old girl some time.

HELEN: The pain we feel, is—Usable.

ANNIE [V.O.] [IRONIC]: Yes, Margaret Fuller.

HELEN: What?

ANNIE [V.O.]: She said, I accept the universe.

HELEN: Yes.

ANNIE [V.O.]: Carlyle said, She'd better.

(They are moving out, hand in hand; music in.)

And also said, All work is as seed sown. If only we didn't have to work!—we could read him—

(Lights fade as they go, ANNIE *with one glance back.)*

William Gibson

has published poetry, plays, fiction, and autobiography; he
is co-author with Margaret Brenman, a psychoanalyst, of
two grown sons.